PUBLIC POLICY APPLICATIONS OF LIFE-CYCLE ASSESSMENT

Edited by

David T. Allen
Frank J. Consoli
Gary A. Davis
James A. Fava
John L. Warren

Proceedings from the Workshop on
Application of Life-Cycle Assessment to Public Policy
14–19 August 1995
Wintergreen, Virginia, USA

SETAC Technical Publications Series

Publication sponsored by the Society of Environmental Toxicology and Chemistry (SETAC) and the SETAC Foundation for Environmental Education

Cover by Michael Kenney Graphic Design and Advertising

Library of Congress Cataloging-in-Publication Data

Pellston Workshop on Application of Life-Cycle Assessment to Public Policy (1995 : Wintergreen, Va.)
  Public policy applications of life-cycle assessment : proceedings from the Pellston Workshop on Application of Life-Cycle Assessment to Public Policy , 14-19 August 1995, Wintergreen, Virginia, USA / edited by David T. Allen ... [et al.].
    p.   cm. -- (SETAC technical publications series)
  "Publication sponsored by the Society of Environmental Toxicology and Chemistry (SETAC) and the SETAC Foundation for Environmental Education."
  Includes bibliographical references (p.).
  ISBN 1-880611-18-X
  1. Environmental management--Congresses. 2. Products life-cycle--Environmental aspects--Congresses. 3. Environmental policy--Congresses. I. Allen, David T. II. SETAC (Organization) III. SETAC Foundation for Environmental Education. IV. Title. V. Series.
GE300.P38 1998
363.7'05--dc21   97-29289
                                                                                                                CIP

Information in this book was obtained from individual experts and highly regarded sources. It is the publisher's intent to print accurate and reliable information, and numerous references are cited; however, the authors, editors, and publisher cannot be responsible for the validity of all information presented here or for the consequences of its use. Information contained herein does not necessarily reflect the policy or views of the Society of Environmental Toxicology and Chemistry (SETAC) or the SETAC Foundation for Environmental Education.

No part of this publication may be reproduced, stored in a retrieval system, or transmitted in any form or by any means, electronic, electrostatic, magnetic tape, mechanical, photocopying, recording, or otherwise, without permission in writing from the copyright holder.

All rights reserved. Authorization to photocopy items for internal or personal use, or the personal or internal use of specific clients, may be granted by the Society of Environmental Toxicology and Chemistry (SETAC), provided that $.50 per page photocopied is paid directly to Copyright Clearance Center, 222 Rosewood Drive, Danvers, MA 01923 USA (telephone 508-750-8400).

SETAC's consent does not extend to copying for general distribution, for promotion, for creating new works, or for resale. Specific permission must be obtained in writing from SETAC for such copying. Direct inquires to the Society of Environmental Toxicology and Chemistry (SETAC), 1010 North 12th Avenue, Pensacola, FL 32501-3370, USA.

© 1997 Society of Environmental Toxicology and Chemistry (SETAC)
Published by Society of Environmental Toxicology and Chemistry
SETAC Press is an imprint of the Society of Environmental Toxicology and Chemistry.
No claim is made to original US. Government works.

International Standard Book Number 1-880611-18-x
Printed in the United States of America
04 03 02 01 00 99 98 97   10 9 8 7 6 5 4 3 2 1

∞The paper used in this publication meets the minimum requirements of the American National Standard for Information Sciences--Permanence of Paper for Printed Library Materials, ANSI Z39.48-1984.

Reference Listing: Allen DT, Consoli FJ, Davis JA, Warren JL, editors. 1997. Public policy applications of life-cycle assessment. Proceedings from the Workshop on Application of Life-Cycle Assessment to Public Policy; 1995 Aug 14-19; Wintergreen, VA. Pensaola Fl: Society of Environmental Toxicology and Chemistry. 138 p.

The SETAC Technical Publication Series

The SETAC Technical Publications Series was established by the Society of Environmental Toxicology and Chemistry (SETAC) to provide in-depth reviews and critical appraisals on scientific subjects relevant to understanding the impacts of chemicals and technology on the environment. The series consists of single- and multiple-authored or edited books on topics reviewed and recommended by the SETAC Board of Directors and approved by the Publications advisory Council for their importance, timeliness, and contribution to multidisciplinary approaches to solving environmental problems. The diversity and breadth of subjects covered in the series reflects the wide range of disciplines encompassed by environmental toxicology, environmental chemistry, and hazard and risk assessment. Despite this diversity, the goals of these volumes are similar; they are to present the reader with authoritative coverage of the literature, as well as paradigms, methodologies and controversies, research needs, and new developments specific to the featured topics.

The SETAC Technical Publications are useful to environmental scientists in research, research management, chemical manufacturing, regulation, and education, as well as to students considering or preparing for careers in these areas. The series provides information for keeping abreast of recent developments in familiar subject areas and for rapid introduction to principles and approaches in new subject areas.

Other Publications by SETAC

Atmospheric Deposition of Contaminants to the Great Lakes and Coastal Waters, edited by Joel E. Baker

Chemically Induced Alterations in Functional Development and Reproduction of Fishes, edited by R.M. Rolland, M. Gilbertson, and R.E. Peterson

Quantitative Structure-Activity Relationships in Environmental Sciences—VII, edited by Fei Chen and Gerrit Schüürmann

Chemical Ranking and Scoring: Guidelines for Relative Assessments of Chemicals, edited by Mary Swanson and Adam Socha

Ecological Risk Assessments of Contaminated Sediments, edited by C. Ingersoll, T. Dillon, and G. Biddinger

For more information about SETAC publications, contact

SETAC
1010 N 12th Avenue
Pensacola, FL 32501 USA
T 850 469 1500 F 850 469 9778 E setac@setac.org
http://www.setac.org

Workshop Participants and Contributing Authors

Eva Ahlner
Swedish Waste Research Council
Stockholm Sweden

David Allen[e]
University of Texas Austin
Austin TX

Michael R. Anderberg
Department of Defense
Washington DC

Jacques Besnainou
Ecobalance, In.
Rockville MD

Kevin Brady
Environment Canada
Hull, Quebec, Canada

Mary T. Campbell
U.S. Environmental Protection Agency
Washington DC

Frank Consoli[e]
Consoli Consulting Company
Media PA

Basil Constantelos
Safety-Kleen Corporation
Elgin IL

Gary Davis[e]
University of Tennessee
Knoxville TN

John Ehrenfeld
Massachusetts Institute of Technology
Cambridge MA

Jim Fava[e]
Roy F. Weston Inc
West Chester PA

William Ferretti
New York State Dept. of Economic Development
Albany NY

Thomas Foust
Department of Energy
Washington, DC

Kathleen Frevert
California Integrated Waste Management Board
Sacramento CA

Paul Geelen
Dutch Ministry of Housing, Spatial Planning, and the Environment
The Hague, The Netherlands

Eun-sook Y. Goidel
U.S. Environmental Protection Agency
Washington DC

Gerald Hane
U.S. House Committee on Science, Space and Technology
Washington DC

Rebecca Hanmer
OECD
Washington DC

Lisa M. Harris
U.S. Environmental Protection Agency
Washington DC

Barbara S. Hill
IBM
Somers NY

Dale Humbert
Midland MI

Kenneth Humphreys
Battelle
Richland WA

Frances H. Irwin
World Resources Institute
Washington DC

Krista Johnsen
National Institute of Science and Technology-MEP
Gaithersburg MD

Larry Laibson
U.S. Army
Dover NJ

Michael H. Levy
Society of the Plastic's Industry
Washington DC

David Monsma
Environmental Action
Tacoma Park MD

Rodney Parrish
SETAC
Pensacola FL

Charles A. Pittinger
The Procter & Gamble Company
Cincinnati OH

Steven D. Pomper
Alcan Aluminum Ltd.
Montreal, Quebec Canada

John Resslar
Saturn Corporation
Troy MI

Stanley Rhodes
Scientific Certification Systems
Oakland CA

Julie Roque
Office of Science, Technology and Policy
Washington DC

Karen Shapiro
Tellus Institute
Boston MA

Robert J. Shimp
The Procter & Gamble Company
Cincinnati OH

Donald R. Theissen
3M Company
St. Paul MN

Susan Thorneloe
U.S. Environmental Protection Agency
Research Triangle Park NC

John Warren[e]
U.S. Environmental Protection Agency
Washington DC

v

Arthur Weissman
Green Seal
Washington DC

John S. Young
Hampshire Research Institute
Alexandria VA

ᵉEditors of this volume

Contents

Executive Summary 1

Chapter 1: Life-Cycle Assessment 7
1.1   Introduction 7
1.2   References 9

Chapter 2: A Conceptual Framework for the Application of the Life-Cycle Concept and Life-Cycle Assessment to Public Policy 11
2.1   Life-cycle concept 11
2.2   Life-cycle concept qualitative to quantitative 13
2.3   Life-cycle assessment 13
2.4   Life-cycle concept and public policy 14
2.5   Systems approach to public policy for the environment 15
2.6   Basic technology decision process and policy instruments 16
    2.6.1   Regulatory policies 18
    2.6.2   Economic and technology policies 19
    2.6.3   Information dissemination and education 20
2.7   Summary 20
2.8   References 20

Chapter 3: Environmental Labeling 21
3.1   Introduction 21
3.2   Background on environmental labeling 21
    3.2.1   Goals of environmental labeling 21
    3.2.2   Types of environmental labeling 22
3.3   Status of life-cycle approaches in environmental labeling 24
    3.3.1   Use of life-cycle approaches in third-party seal-of-approval programs .. 24
    3.3.2   Use of life-cycle approaches in specific claims declarations 25
    3.3.3   Use of LCA in quantitative environmental information labeling ... 28
3.4   Framework for the use of life-cycle approaches in environmental labeling 28
3.5   Technical assessment of the application of life-cycle approaches to environmental labeling 31

  3.5.1 Tools for life-cycle approaches in environmental labeling programs 31
  3.5.2 Technical issues in quantitative LCA in environmental labeling 35
  3.5.3 Strengths and weaknesses of more qualitative versus more quantitative approaches in environmental labeling 37
3.6 Measuring the effectiveness of life-cycle approaches in ecolabeling programs 38
  3.6.1 Why measure? 39
  3.6.2 Who measures? 39
  3.6.3 What should be measured: specific issues to address in a performance review 39
  3.6.4 Timing of the performance review 40
3.7 Stakeholder involvement in the use of life-cycle approaches in environmental labeling 40
3.8 Communication of life-cycle approaches used in environmental labeling programs 42
  3.8.1 Generic communications requirements 42
  3.8.2 Third-party seal-of-approval programs 43
  3.8.3 Specific claims declarations 43
  3.8.4 Quantified product information labels 43
3.9 Conclusions and recommendations 43
3.10 References 44

Chapter 4: Acquisition and Procurement 47

4.1 Introduction 47
  4.1.1 Scope 47
  4.1.2 Definitions 47
  4.1.3 Environmental considerations in the acquisition process 48
  4.1.4 Stakeholders 48
  4.1.5 The role of life-cycle concepts in acquisition and procurement 48
4.2 General concepts and issues 49
  4.2.1 Who is a stakeholder? 49
  4.2.2 Consensus 51
  4.2.3 Valuation 52
  4.2.4 The unique nature of the customer in public procurement 53
  4.2.5 Interdependence of stakeholders, consensus, and valuation 54
  4.2.6 Win-win opportunities 54
  4.2.7 Simplicity vs. complexity 55
  4.2.8 Small business considerations 55
4.3 Acquisition 55
  4.3.1 A closer look at an acquisition process the DoD process 56
  4.3.2 System engineering approach the Saturn example 59
4.4 Procurement of environmentally preferable products and services 60

	4.4.1 Goal	60
	4.4.2 Environmentally preferred products and services	60
	4.4.3 Issues	67
4.5	Conceptual toolbox methods: applicable to acquisition and procurement	68
	4.5.1 Tools used in the acquisition process	68
	4.5.2 Tools applicable to procurement decisions	69
	4.5.3 Economic accounting tools	69
	4.5.4 Non-economic metrics used in analysis	70
4.6	Implementation	71
4.7	Summary of key findings	73
4.8	Future needs	74
	4.8.1 Acquisition	74
	4.8.2 Procurement	74
	4.8.3 Tools and metrics	74
4.9	References	75

Chapter 5: Policy and Regulations ... 77

5.1	Goals of using life-cycle concepts in public policy	77
	5.1.1 Goal	77
	5.1.2 Observations	78
5.2	Generic framework for applying life-cycle concepts to public policy	79
5.3	Case study comparison of municipal solid waste management options using a life-cycle assessment	80
	5.3.1 Background	80
	5.3.2 Purpose	81
	5.3.3 Definition of the problem	81
	5.3.4 Limitations of conventional approaches	81
	5.3.5 Value of life-cycle concepts to address this problem	82
	5.3.6 Obstacles	83
	5.3.7 Overcoming obstacles	84
	5.3.8 Communication	84
5.4	Case study: USEPA waste minimization and combustion strategy	85
	5.4.1 Introduction	85
	5.4.2 Purpose	85
	5.4.3 Limitations of conventional approach	85
	5.4.4 Value of life-cycle concepts	86
	5.4.5 Obstacles	86
	5.4.6 Overcoming obstacles	87
5.5	Case study USEPA industrial laundries effluent guideline	87

	5.5.1 Background 87
	5.5.2 Purpose 88
	5.5.3 Limitations of conventional approach 88
	5.5.4 Value of life-cycle concepts 88
	5.5.5 Obstacles and overcoming obstacles 90
	5.5.6 Communication 90
5.6	Case study: incorporating LCA concepts in a degreasing rule 91
	5.6.1 Background 91
	5.6.2 Purpose 91
	5.6.3 Limitations of conventional approach 91
	5.6.4 Value of life-cycle concepts 92
	5.6.5 Applying life-cycle concepts 92
	5.6.6 Obstacles 92
	5.6.7 Lessons learned 93
5.7	Case study: Dutch system for continuous environmental improvements in consumer products 93
	5.7.1 Background 93
	5.7.2 Purpose 93
	5.7.3 Limitations of conventional approach 94
	5.7.4 Value of life-cycle concepts 94
	5.7.5 Obstacles 95
	5.7.6 Overcoming obstacles 96
	5.7.7 Communication 97
	5.7.8 Summary 97
5.8	Barriers 98
	5.8.1 Lack of education 98
	5.8.2 Lack of acceptance of life-cycle concepts as decision-making tools 99
	5.8.3 Lack of stakeholder participation / partnerships 99
	5.8.4 Requirements for data confidentiality 100
	5.8.5 Difficulty in defining scope / boundaries 100
	5.8.6 Shortage of time and resources and inability to reduce costs 101
	5.8.7 Lack of tools and data 101
5.9	LCA in strategic policy planning: international perspectives 101
5.10	Observations and recommendations 103
	5.10.1 Observations 103
	5.10.2 Recommendations 103
5.11	References 104

Chapter 6: Environmental Technology 115
6.1	Introduction 105
	6.1.1 Overview: technology, public policy, and life-cycle concepts 105
	6.1.2 Definitions 105

		6.1.3	Relationship of technology to public policy	106
		6.1.4	Relationship of LCA to public policy	106
		6.1.5	Using LCA in policy to promote environmental technology	107
		6.1.6	Integration framework	108
	6.2	A framework for the use of life-cycle concepts in public policy		111
		6.2.1	Introduction: some policy considerations and principles	111
		6.2.2	Research, development, and demonstration policy	112
		6.2.3	Regulatory policy (U.S.)	113
		6.2.4	Market stimulus (market-based) policies	113
		6.2.5	Fiscal policy	114
		6.2.6	International commerce & foreign aid	114
		6.2.7	Education and training	115
		6.2.8	Information dissemination	115
	6.3	Life-cycle applications to public policy for environmental technology		116
	6.4	Life-cycle applications in public policy development		118
		6.4.1	Study introduction and purpose	118
		6.4.2	Case studies examined	118
		6.4.3	Results and discussion	121
		6.4.4	LCA as a tool in forming environmental public policy	123
		6.4.5	Key Findings	126
	6.5	References		127

List of Figures

Figure 2-1	Life-cycle concept	12
Figure 2-2	Life-cycle continuum	13
Figure 3-1	Life-cycle approach applied to environmental labeling	29
Figure 3-2	European Union ecolabeling and LCA steps	35
Figure 4-1	Traditional approach: acquisition and procurement decision	50
Figure 4-2	Strategic approach: acquisition and procurement decision	51
Figure 5-1	Life-cycle flows	83
Figure 5-2	Material and energy flows in a unit operation	84
Figure 5-3	Life-cycle inventory template	87
Figure 5-4	Industrial laundering process	89
Figure 6-1	Integration framework: technology, public policy, LCA	109
Figure 6-2	LCA type and application	122
Figure 6-3	Information dissemination orientation	123
Figure 6-4	Research, development, and demonstration orientation	124
Figure 6-5	Market stimulation orientation	125
Figure 6-6	Regulatory orientation	126

List of Tables

Table 1-1	SETAC-sponsored LCA workshops	8
Table 3-1	Methods used to award	26
Table 4-1	Example non-cost metrics for life-cycle	71
Table 6-1	Public sector LCA studies	119

Executive Summary

The life-cycle concept is a "cradle-to-grave" systems approach for analyzing environmental impacts of products, services, or activities. The concept is based on the recognition that all life-cycle stages along with all steps of development cycles result in economic, environmental, and energy impacts (see Figure 1). Understanding the interaction of life-cycle stages and development steps yields a better understanding of the consequences of technology choices. Historically, the negative consequences associated with technology choices have often been overlooked when a life-cycle concept has not been employed.

> The life-cycle concept is a powerful systems approach for thinking about technology from a "cradle-to-grave" perspective. Life-cycle assessment (LCA) is one analytical tool for implementing life-cycle concepts. Use of life-cycle concepts and tools can link scientific, technological, and policy-making communities in an overall effort to find an appropriate balance between economic, environmental, and energy considerations.

More specifically, the life-cycle concept is based on recognition of the following:
- A "cradle-to-grave" perspective is important to any evaluation. More site-specific, "end-of-the-pipe," "within-the-plant-gate," or "end-of-product-life" perspectives may be limiting because they do not recognize the full range of upstream and downstream implications of site-specific actions.
- For any technology (product, service, or activity), material, energy, labor, and monetary demands are placed upon raw material acquisition; manufacturing, processing, and formulation; transportation and distribution; use, reuse, and maintenance; and recycling and waste management processes across the continent and around the world. Further, each of these processes may result in indirect economic, environmental, and energy impacts.
- Temporal and spatial dimensions to economic, environmental, and energy impacts should be considered.
- An inherently integrative concept, such as the life-cycle concept, is the best way to allow for the evaluation of economic, environmental, and energy dimensions of a problem at the same time.

The life-cycle concept is being implemented through a wide variety of approaches, such as those shown in Figure 2. The life-cycle concept may be implemented quantitatively. It may also be implemented qualitatively by using the concept to logically think through the economic, environmental, and energy implications of technology choices. The approaches in Figure 2, along with other approaches that can be coupled with them (e.g., risk assessment), create a

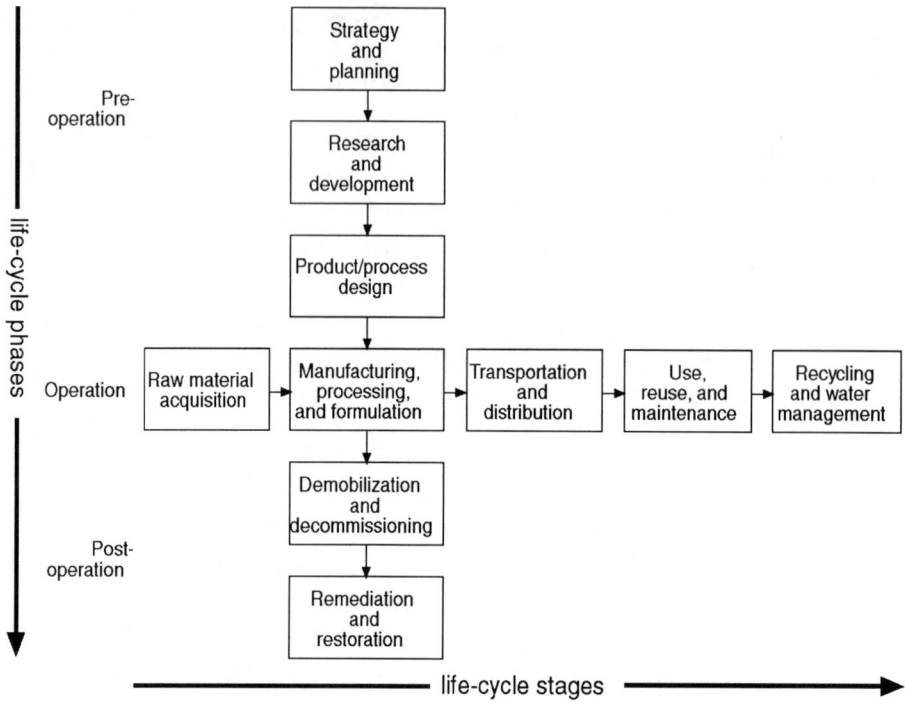

Figure 1 Life-cycle concept

"toolbox" of analytic approaches that are available to comprehensively evaluate environmental technologies.

Life-cycle assessment

Life-cycle assessment (LCA), an evolving quantitative tool, incorporates the life-cycle concept into an analytical framework that has three quantitative elements, in addition to a goal identification and scoping exercise. The first element is a life-cycle inventory analysis, which quantitatively evaluates the environmental and energy stressors associated with a product, service, or activity by identifying and quantifying energy and materials used and residuals produced over its entire life cycle. The second element is a life-cycle impact assessment, which evaluates the impact of these energy and material uses and releases to the environment. The third element is a life-cycle improvement assessment, which identifies and evaluates opportunities to affect environmental improvements.

Life-cycle assessment
- quantifies the energy use, material requirements, wastes, emissions, and environmental impacts that are associated with the provision of a product, service, or activity throughout its life cycle.
- contributes to a quantitative understanding of the overall and interdependent nature of environmental consequences and human activities.

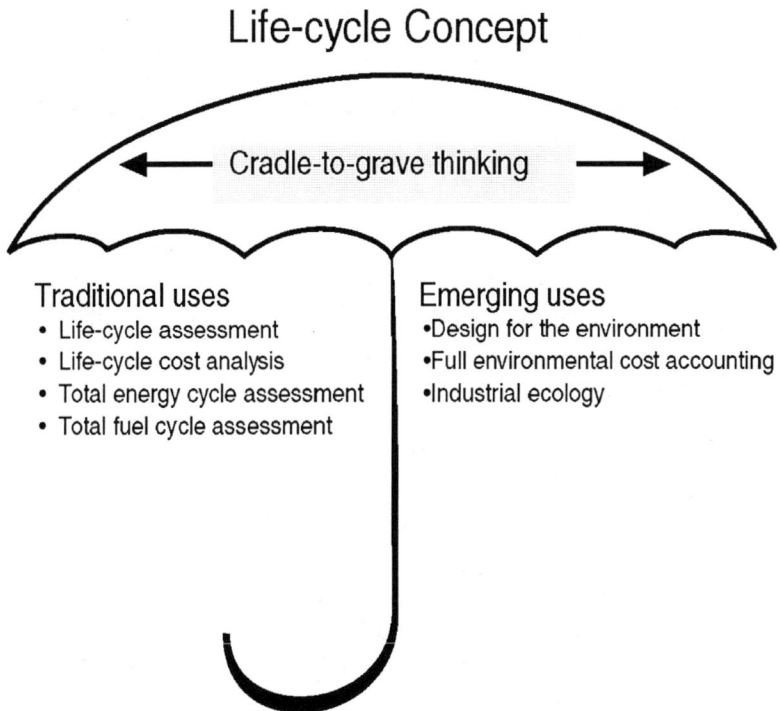

Figure 2   Example approaches: incorporating life-cycle concept

- provides decision-makers with quantitative information that describes the known environmental effects associated with the provision of products, services, and activities, and identifies opportunities for environmental improvements and highlights data gaps.

Life-cycle concept and public policy

The life-cycle concept may improve the public policy process by providing information to decision-makers in a comprehensive manner. Public policy decisions, however, are extremely varied. They range from the implementation of narrow mandates to the development of broad policy statements and involve very different institutions, from local planning departments to federal agencies and the Executive Office of the President. Consequently, the application of the life-cycle concept to public policy will involve a broad range of depth, breadth, and rigor. All life-cycle assessments, from back-of-the-envelope calculations to very comprehensive and precise analyses, should take a cradle-to-grave perspective.

A systems approach to public policy for the environment

The life-cycle concept can improve environmental policy-making by assessing integrated environmental, energy, and economic issues. Its use will support ongoing efforts of environmental policy-makers in moving from fragmented end-of-the-pipe and end-of-product-life approaches toward more integrated approaches that reflect technology and environmental systems.

Experimental projects have documented the need for new policy approaches and the possibilities of developing them. The Blackstone project in Massachusetts demonstrated the potential of integrated facility inspections both to use staff resources more effectively and to stimulate greater use of pollution prevention. The Amoco-U.S. Environmental Protection Agency (USEPA) project illustrated the potential of strategic environmental assessment at the facility level to improve environmental data and to identify options that provide the most prevention or protection at the least cost. Pilot projects currently underway in the USEPA, the Department of Defense, the Department of Energy, and in a number of states are probing the value of the life-cycle concept in a variety of policy settings.

The life-cycle concept and associated assessment tools are thus entering a fertile terrain of integrated perspectives and tools. In focusing on the choice of technology or product, life cycle as a concept and as a tool promises to be particularly effective for moving consideration of environmental impacts upstream to research and development (R&D) and purchasing decisions, where impacts can be more easily avoided or mitigated at a lower cost.

> ### Stimulating markets for environmentally preferable products
> Executive Order 12873 mandates the procurement of environmentally preferable goods and services by federal agencies. The order harnesses the federal government's purchasing power of over $200 billion per year to promote the acquisition of products that result in less risk to human and ecological health. The USEPA will use the life-cycle concept to establish guidelines for the procurement process. Life-cycle concepts offer a holistic and comprehensive perspective that is necessary to address the complex issues in identifying environmentally preferable products. No other analysis tool provides this perspective.

Recommendations for further action

The life-cycle concept is being applied in a number of pilot projects utilizing a range of policy instruments. These efforts should be expanded. Further, a comprehensive plan for evaluating, comparing, and disseminating the results of these studies should be created and implemented.

For life-cycle concepts to be widely applied in policy settings, the results must be understandable, transparent, and accessible to all stakeholders. This level of understanding will require an aggressive education and information-dissemination effort that is not currently in place. Universities, government, industry, and environmental advocacy groups should form partnerships to improve understanding of the life-cycle concept and accessibility to the results of life-cycle studies.

For more information about the workshop and the Society of Environmental Toxicology and Chemistry (SETAC) publications on LCA, fax the SETAC Office at 904 469 9778 or call Rod Parrish, Executive Director, SETAC/SETAC Foundation for Environmental Education at 904 469 1500. The SETAC Office address is 1010 North 12th Avenue, Pensacola, Florida 32501-3370.

Chapter 1
Life-Cycle Assessment

1.1 Introduction

Increased awareness and concern over environmental impacts has renewed interest in methods to understand the consequences of human activities on the environment. In recent years, the idea that environmental assessment methods must encourage a comprehensive evaluation of all "upstream" and "downstream" effects of the activity or product under examination has gained acceptance. This life-cycle or "cradle-to-grave" concept, has influenced many approaches to calculate, assess, and improve the environmental performance of products and production systems.

One of the more recognized methods for examining environmental performance is life-cycle assessment (LCA). Life-cycle assessment is a process to evaluate the environmental burdens associated with a product, process, or activity by identifying and quantifying energy and materials used and wastes released to the environment; to assess the potential impact of those energy and material uses and releases to the environment; and to identify and evaluate opportunities to affect environmental improvements. The assessment is designed to include the entire life cycle of the product, process, or activity, encompassing extracting and processing raw materials; manufacturing; transportation and distribution; use, reuse, maintenance; recycling, and final disposal (Fava et al. 1991).

Life-cycle assessment addresses potential environmental impacts of the system under study in the areas of ecological health, human health, and resource depletion. It does not address economic considerations or social effects. Additionally, like all other scientific models, LCA is a simplification of the physical system and cannot claim to provide an absolute and complete representation of every environmental interaction.

The prime objectives of carrying out a LCA are
1) to provide as complete a picture as possible of the interactions of an activity with the environment;
2) to contribute to the understanding of the overall and interdependent nature of the environmental consequences of human activities; and
3) to provide decision-makers with information which defines the potential environmental impacts of these activities and identifies opportunities for environmental improvements.

Additionally, the systematic procedures for LCA facilitate constructive dialogue among sectors in society concerned with environmental quality. Life-cycle concepts can also have an important influence on a range of techniques and thought processes that guide decision-making and the selection of options for design and improvement.

Table 1-1   SETAC-sponsored LCA workshops

Topic	Site	Date	Report
A technical framework for LCA	Smugglers Notch, Vermont USA	18–23 Aug 1990	Fava et al. 1991
Life-cycle assessment	Leiden, The Netherlands	2–3 Dec 1991	
A conceptual framework for LCA impact assessment	Sandestin, Florida USA	1–6 Feb 1992	Fava et al. 1993
LCA data quality: A conceptual framework	Wintergreen, Virginia USA	4–9 Oct 1992	Fava et al. 1994
Guidelines for LCA: a "code of practice"	Sesimbra, Portugal	Mar 1993	Consoli et al. 1993
Applications of LCA to public policy	Wintergreen, Virginia USA	14–19 Aug 1994	This work

Work to develop broad consensus on the conduct of LCA was initiated in 1990 by the Society of Environmental Toxicology and Chemistry (SETAC). A series of workshops convening representatives of the international LCA community has produced documents reflecting consensus and current thinking on the practice of LCA (Table 1-1).

These documents have charted the development of LCA, primarily as a tool for industry to assess and improve the environmental performance of their products, processes or activities. Recent trends, however, in the use of LCA have shifted into the public arena.

Within Europe and elsewhere, LCA has become the basis for product labeling procedures. In the United States, LCA has been suggested as a tool for establishing procurement standards, and as a framework for analyzing environmental regulation.

LCA holds great promise as a tool to help decision-makers (both public and private) make more informed decisions regarding the environment, but given the state of development of LCA and its inherent limitations, broad public policy use will be difficult. Clearly, what is needed is a framework for properly using LCA together with other analysis tools in environmental policy decisions.

In August of 1994, SETAC sponsored this workshop, Applications of Life-Cycle Assessment to Public Policy, to define a framework for the use of LCA in public policy decision-making. The objectives of the workshop were to

- define the public policy arenas in which LCA could inform decision-making,

Chapter 1: Introduction

- develop specific guidance for the use of LCA in public policy,
- specify a framework and approach for LCA use in public policy decisions, and
- determine future research needs in the application of LCA to public policy-making.

Approximately 40 internationally recognized experts in LCA and the application of LCA to public policy-making were organized into 5 working groups. One working group was charged with outlining a framework for the application of life-cycle assessment to public policy. Their report is contained in Chapter 2. The remaining 4 groups considered specific application arenas. Chapter 3 reports on the use of LCA in environmental labeling initiatives. Chapter 4 examines the use of LCA in governmental acquisition and procurement. Chapter 5 considers the use of LCA in analyzing regulations and setting policy, and Chapter 6 probes the use of LCA in identifying environmental technologies.

1.2 References

Consoli F, Allen D, Boustead I, Fava J, Franklin W, Jensen A, de Oude N, Parrish R, Perriman R, Postlethwaite D, Quay B, Séguin J, Vigon B, editors. 1993. Guidelines for life-cycle assessment. Pensacola FL: SETAC Pr.

Fava J, Denison R, Jones B, Curran MA, Vigon B, Selke S, Barnum J, editors. 1991. A technical framework for life-cycle assessment. Society of Environmental Toxicology and Chemistry (SETAC) Pellston Workshop; 1990 Aug 18–23; Smuggler's Notch VT. Pensacola FL: SETAC Pr.

Fava J, Consoli F, Denison R, Dickson K, Mohin T, Vigon B, editors. 1993. Conceptual framework for impact assessment. Society of Environmental Toxicology and Chemistry (SETAC) Pellston Workshop; 1992 Feb 1–6; Sandestin FL. Pensacola FL: SETAC Pr.

Fava J, Jensen AA, Lindfors L, Pomper S, DeSmet B, Warren J, Vigon B, editors. 1994. Life-cycle assessment data quality: a conceptual framework. Society of Environmental Toxicology and Chemistry (SETAC) Pellston Workshop on Life-Cycle Data Quality; 1992 Oct 4–9; Wintergreen VA. Pensacola FL: SETAC Pr.

SETAC Press

Chapter 2
A Conceptual Framework for the Application of the Life-Cycle Concept and Life-Cycle Assessment to Public Policy

2.1 Life-cycle concept

The life-cycle concept is a "cradle-to-grave" systems approach for thinking about technology. The concept is based on the recognition that all life-cycle stages (raw material acquisition; manufacturing, processing, and formulation; transportation and distribution; use, reuse, and maintenance; and recycling and waste management) along with all life-cycle phases (pre-operation, operation, and post-operation) result in economic, environmental, and energy impacts (see Figure 2-1). Understanding all life-cycle stages and phases can yield a better understanding of the consequences of technology choices. Without consideration of life-cycle concepts, unforeseen negative consequences may be overlooked.

> The life-cycle concept is a powerful systems approach for thinking about technology from a "cradle-to-grave" perspective. Life-cycle assessment (LCA) is one type of analytical tool for implementing the life-cycle concept.

More specifically, the life-cycle concept is based on a recognition of the following:

- A "cradle-to-grave" perspective is important to any evaluation. More site-specific, "end-of-the-pipe," "within-the-plant-gate," or "end-of-product-life" perspectives may be limiting because they do not recognize the full range of upstream and downstream implications of site-specific actions.

- For any technology (product, service, or activity), material, energy, labor, and monetary demands are placed upon raw material acquisition, manufacturing, processing, formulation, transportation, distribution, use, reuse, maintenance, and recycling and waste management processes across the continent and around the world. Further, each of these processes may result in indirect economic, environmental, and energy impacts.

- Temporal and spatial dimensions to economic, environmental, and energy impacts should be considered.

- An inherently integrative concept, such as the life-cycle concept, is the best way to allow for the evaluation of economic, environmental, and energy dimensions of a problem at the same time.

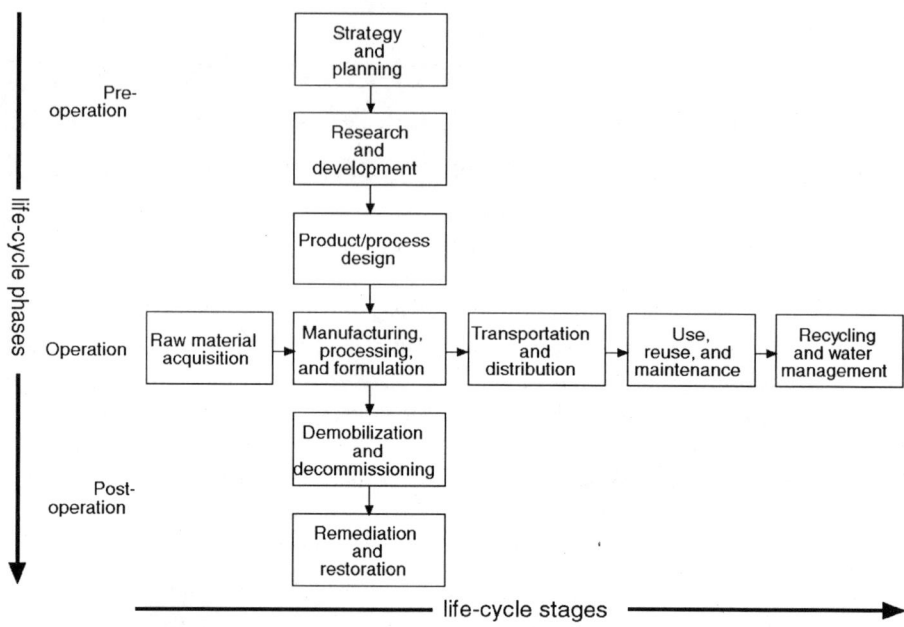

Figure 2-1   Life-cycle concept

Life-cycle assessment
- quantifies the energy use, material requirements, wastes, emissions, and potential environmental impacts that are associated with the provision of a product, service, or activity throughout its life cycle.
- contributes to a quantitative understanding of the overall and interdependent nature of environmental consequences and human activities.
- provides decision-makers with quantitative information that describes the potential environmental effects associated with the provision of products, services, and activities and identifies opportunities for environmental improvements and highlights data gaps.
- does not address economic considerations or social effects (Consoli et al. 1993), although it may be used in conjunction with other quantitative tools to address these issues.

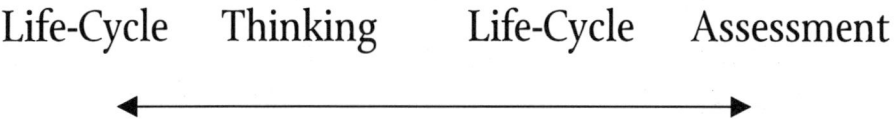

Figure 2-2   Life-cycle continuum

> State of development of LCA methodology
> - Goal definition and scoping is defined.
> - Inventory analysis is defined and understood, but would benefit from refinement.
> - Impact assessment is defined conceptually with multiple techniques in use, but needs further development.
> - Improvement assessment has techniques in use, but is not yet documented.

2.2 Life-cycle concept qualitative to quantitative

Classifying a comprehensive LCA as a very quantitative approach and life-cycle thinking as the most basic, qualitative approach that still embodies the life-cycle concept, a continuum is established (Figure 2-2).

Along this continuum (moving left to right) lie increasingly more comprehensive assessment approaches (as measured by depth, breadth, and rigor).

The life-cycle concept has been implemented through a wide variety of approaches, and is also being used in an emerging set of tools (Figure 2-3). The life-cycle concept may be implemented quantitatively. It may also be implemented qualitatively by using the concept to logically think through the economic, environmental, and energy implications of technology choices. The approaches shown in Figure 2-3, along with other approaches that can be coupled with them (e.g., risk assessment), create a "toolbox" of analytic approaches that are available to comprehensively evaluate environmental technologies.

2.3 Life-cycle assessment

Life-cycle assessment incorporates the life-cycle concept into an analytical framework that has three quantitative elements, in addition to a goal identification and scoping exercise.

As outlined earlier, the first element is a life-cycle inventory analysis, which quantitatively evaluates the environmental and energy stressors associated with

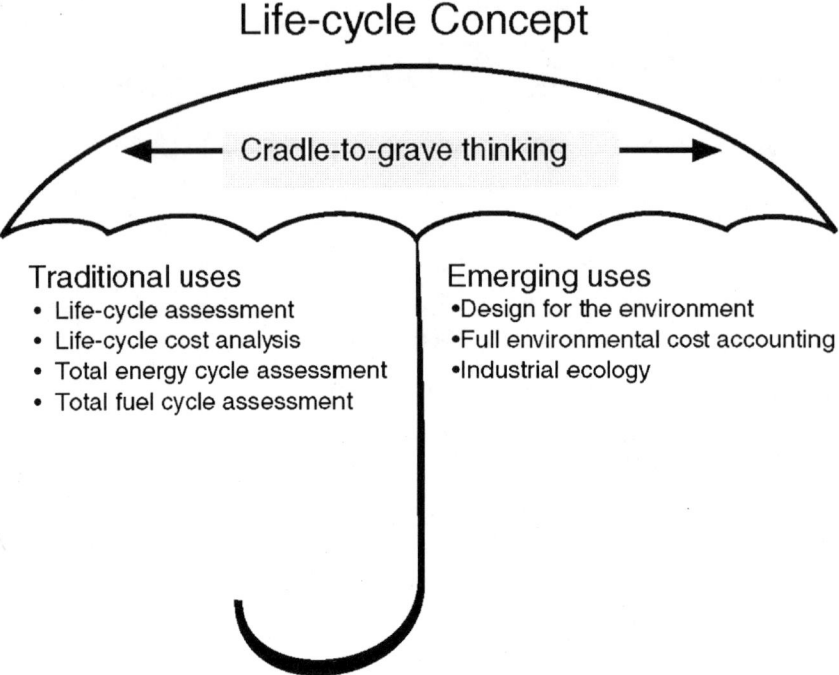

Figure 2-3   Approaches that incorporate the life-cycle concept

a product, service, or activity by identifying and quantifying energy and materials used and residuals produced over its entire life cycle. The second element is a life-cycle impact assessment, which evaluates the potential impact of these energy and material uses and releases to the environment. The third element is a life-cycle improvement assessment, which identifies and evaluates opportunities to affect environmental improvements.

2.4 Life-cycle concept and public policy

Application of the life-cycle concept may improve the public policy process by providing more information to decision-makers in a comprehensive manner. Public policy decisions, however, are extremely varied. They range from the implementation of narrow mandates to the development of broad policy statements and involve very different institutions from local planning departments to federal agencies and the Executive Office of the President. Consequently, the application of the life-cycle concept to public policy will involve a broad range of depth, breadth and rigor.

Further considerations in applying LCA to public policy are listed below.
- LCAs should be framed appropriately and boundaries for the analysis should be drawn to reflect policy goals.

- Administrative or legal requirements for the performance of LCAs should retain flexibility to incorporate new scientific advances and data. LCA methodology should continue to evolve and public policy decisions should incorporate state-of-the-art assessments whenever possible.
- The depth or extent of the analysis should be commensurate with the nature and significance of the policy decision.
- The limitations of LCA must be evaluated when decisions based on the assessments are considered.

> Definition of public policy
>
> Public policies are actions, decisions, statements, mandates, orders, or guidance taken by governmental entities that affect other governmental entities, nongovernmental entities, the public, and private interests.
>
> Public policies are shaped and constrained by many interests within and outside government, existing policies, legal and societal norms, and institutional arrangements.
>
> Governmental entities include all regulatory and nonregulatory institutions (e.g., programs, agencies, departments) at local, state, regional, provincial, federal, and international levels, across executive, legislative, and judicial branches

2.5 Systems approach to public policy for the environment

In order to appreciate how the application of the life-cycle concept may improve environmental policy-making, it is first helpful to briefly review the history and status of environmental policy.

For more than a decade, environmental policy-makers have been struggling to move from fragmented end-of-the-pipe and end-of-product-life approaches toward more integrated approaches that reflect the complexity of technology and environmental systems.

Pollution prevention, priority-setting for risk reduction, whole facility, cross-media, and landscape or watershed approaches are among many examples of overlapping efforts to move toward a systems approach.

Pilot projects have documented the need for new policy approaches and the possibilities of developing them. The Blackstone project in Massachusetts demonstrated the potential of integrated facility inspections to both use staff resources more effectively and to stimulate greater use of pollution prevention (Roy and Dillard 1990). The Amoco–USEPA (Amoco-USEPA 1992) project illustrated the potential of strategic environmental assessment at the facility level to improve environmental data and identify options that provide the most prevention or protection at the least cost.

The shift toward more integrative public policy tools is occurring at all levels of government and around the world. At the local level in the U.S., communities and industrial facilities use public, multimedia data on toxic chemicals as the basis for communication or negotiation. Guidance for national governments interested in establishing similar facility pollution registers is now being developed through a series of international workshops. The facility is also the integrative focus for the European Union's eco-management and audit regulation while the product is the focus of its ecolabeling program. Germany's take-back program also focuses on the product. As environment ministers committed to a significant reduction in the pollution load in the 1990s, the Organization for Economic Cooperation (OECD) reorganized its own pollution work, and member countries adopted an OECD act recommending use of integrated pollution prevention and control tools and integrated institutions.

The life-cycle concept and associated assessment tools are thus entering a fertile terrain of integrated perspectives and tools. In focusing on the choice of technology or product, life-cycle promises to be a particularly effective concept and tool for moving consideration of environmental impacts upstream to R&D and purchasing decisions where impacts can be more easily avoided or mitigated at lower cost.

In addition to moving policy selection upstream, life cycle offers a framework which can organize information developed by other tools such as risk assessment or pollution prevention planning that focus on narrower questions. It can also frame the relationships between natural resource and pollution and between energy and materials questions both of which are now usually addressed separately.

2.6 Basic technology decision process and policy instruments

All available options should be examined and evaluated in developing public policies to manage environmental hazards. One means to identify policy instruments is to analyze decisions that lead to adverse health and environmental effects. A method for mapping such decisions is presented as Figure 2-4.

Individuals, companies, the government, and other organizations participate in this basic technology decision process (Figure 2-4) every day. At the most basic level, this is the decision process into which policy will intervene if the government is to help facilitate equitable decisions that balance economics, environmental, and energy considerations.

This decision model enables one to identify strategies to intervene at various points along the chain in order to avoid potentially adverse consequences. While some governmental agencies, such as USEPA, have undertaken initiatives to alter consumer choices ("modify wants") and have encouraged the development of

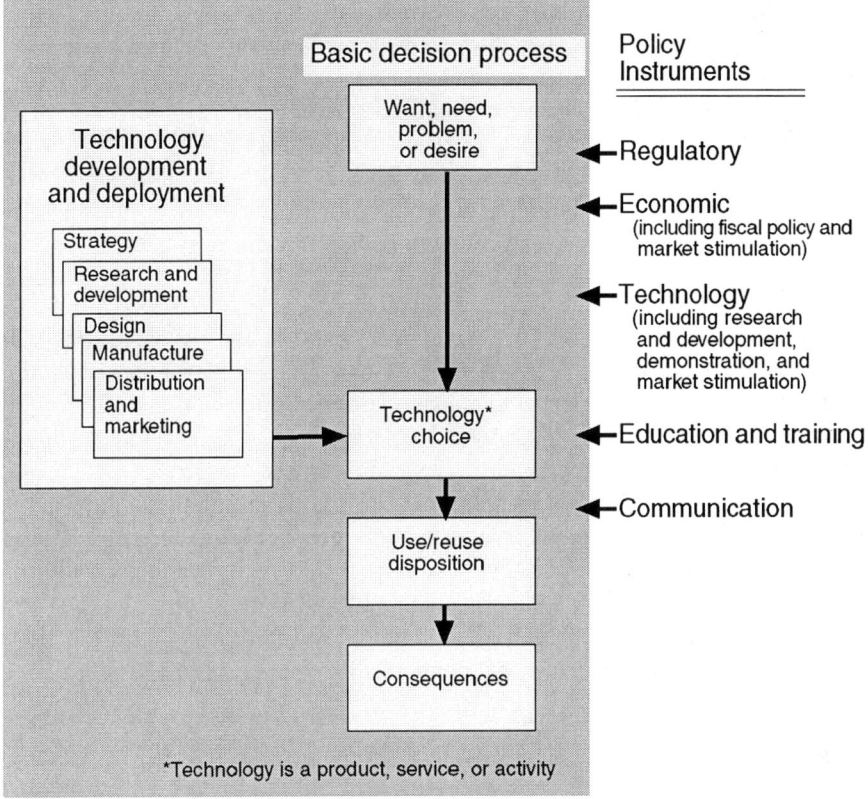

Figure 2-4   Basic technology decision process

alternative technologies, most environmental, occupational and consumer regulations intervene at later stages, at the points of reducing emissions or exposures.

A wide range of policy instruments have been used in the United States as means to manage the environmental impacts associated with the production and consumption of goods. Five categories of policy instruments that may be especially relevant to consider are discussed below. The categories of instruments (Figure 2-5) are

- regulatory policy,
- economic policy (including fiscal policy and market stimulation),
- technology policy (including R&D and demonstration),
- education and training, and
- information dissemination (including communication).

Specific policy instruments that intervene at different points in the causal chain can be identified for most of these categories. Surcharges on consumer products may be intended to discourage the use of particular products, for example, while taxes on manufacturing wastes may affect industrial decisions. Both of these sorts of interventions are economic policy but are aimed at intervening at different points along the causal chain. Examples and discussion are presented below to illustrate what type of specific policy instruments fall within each of the major policy instrument categories and how LCA may be employed in designing the policy instruments. The discussion, however, is not intended to imply that the life-cycle concept will definitively work with any particular instrument.

2.6.1 Regulatory policies

Direct regulations form the backbone of our current system of environmental management and can be used to intervene at most points of the causal chain. Direct regulations are policy instruments that include traditional command-and-control regulations intended to limit loadings of stressors to the environment. Standards based on "acceptable" levels of exposure or discharge rates established for limiting ambient air and water pollution, as well as occupational exposures, fall into this category. Restrictions on the uses of specific high risk chemicals and on particular waste management methods are other means to regulate directly the generation and use of hazardous materials. Direct regulations also can be imposed at other points in the causal chain, such as by requiring producers to change their technology choices or by altering consumer choices by regulating products.

As described in Chapter 5, LCA can be used to inform the development of these regulations. Specific examples considered in the chapter include the use of life-cycle thinking to compare options for managing municipal solid waste and the use of LCA in developing effluent guidelines for industrial laundries, particularly considering the trade-offs between the use of washable and disposable rags in industrial operations.

Planning and reporting requirements are other forms of regulatory policies most often imposed on producers as a means to intervene by encouraging changes in technology choices or reducing stressors. Most of the major federal environmental legislation requires waste generators to report discharges to various media (air, water, or land). Such requirements are intended to increase awareness (in both industry and consumers) of the environmental emissions from technologies and products, and to provide accountability.

Life-cycle assessment can provide a framework for some reporting. As described in Chapter 5, the Dutch government has initiated a program that intends to provide life-cycle data to consumers on many products in the marketplace.

Chapter 2: A Conceptual Framework

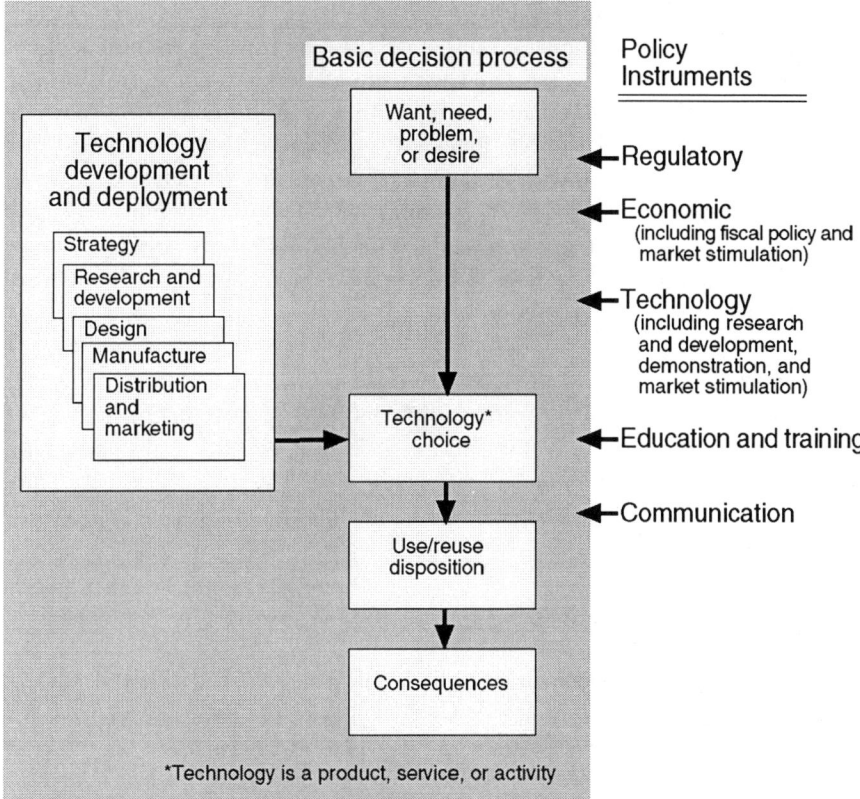

Figure 2-5   Policy instruments

2.6.2 Economic and technology policies

Other governmental attempts to affect both industrial and consumer decisions about environmental impacts, energy or raw material use include the provision of both positive and negative economic incentives that favor particular technologies or products. Negative economic incentives increase the costs of businesses or of consuming products. These include policies to hold sources liable for harm associated with the materials they use, produce or dispose of. In contrast, positive economic incentive programs include governmental procurement giving advantages to environmentally preferable products, the provision of technical assistance, government sponsored research and development of new technologies, and financial assistance in the form of grants, low interest loans, and tax credits. The use of LCA in identifying environmental technologies is described in Chapter 6 and its use in identifying environmentally preferable products for governmental procurement is described in Chapter 4.

2.6.3 Information dissemination and education

The dissemination of information is another method by which government agencies attempt to affect hazards associated with production and consumption. The rationale for these efforts is founded in a belief that both producers and consumers ought to make informed choices, and that information about the health and environmental risks associated with certain products or their manufacture, as well as their substitutes, will encourage the manufacture and use of environmentally preferable products. Product environmental labeling initiatives are a common vehicle for disseminating environmental information. The use of LCA in environmental labeling is discussed in Chapter 3.

2.7 Summary

As described above, the role of the life-cycle concept and LCA in the vast array of policy instruments is being explored through a number case studies and pilot programs. The remaining chapters of this volume will describe these case studies and pilot programs and will attempt to generalize the lessons learned.

2.8 References

Amoco-USEPA Pollution Prevention Project, Project Summary (Available through NTIS) Document PB92-228527, June 1992.

Consoli F, Allen D, Boustead I, Fava J, Franklin W, Jensen A, de Oude N, Parrish R, Perriman R, Postlethwaite D, Quay B, Séguin J, Vigon B, editors. 1993. Guidelines for life-cycle assessment: a "code of practice." Society of Environmental Toxicology and Chemistry (SETAC) and SETAC-Europe Workshop; 1993 Mar; Sesimbra Portugal. Pensacola FL: SETAC Pr.

Roy M, Dillard LA. 1990. Toxics use reduction in Massachusetts: The Blackstone Project. *Journal Air and Waste Management Association* 40:1368–1371.

Chapter 3
Environmental Labeling

3.1 Introduction

The purpose of this chapter is to discuss the use of life-cycle approaches in environmental labeling. The use of environmental labeling in the consumer marketplace has become increasingly widespread. The use of different life-cycle approaches as tools for identifying and evaluating the environmental aspects of products varies widely among current programs, although most embrace the life-cycle concept.

This chapter is organized around the following questions:
- What are the overall goals of environmental labeling, and what is the goal of using life-cycle approaches in the labeling process?
- What life-cycle approaches are being employed today in environmental labeling programs?
- What expectations should there be with respect to the use of different life-cycle approaches in environmental labeling?
- What are the strengths, weaknesses, and limitations of different approaches, and what key technical issues need to be addressed in order for different approaches to be used effectively?
- How can we assess the effectiveness of LCA as it is used in the context of environmental labeling?
- How should stakeholders be involved in environmental labeling programs that utilize life-cycle approaches?
- How can the results of a LCA be most effectively communicated to decision-makers, whether that decision-maker is an environmental labeling authority, or a consumer?

3.2 Background on environmental labeling

In order to understand how life-cycle approaches can be effectively applied to environmental labeling, it is first important to broadly understand the goals of labeling and to define the different types of environmental labeling programs used today in the marketplace.

3.2.1 Goals of environmental labeling

Among the goals of environmental labeling are: 1) to stimulate changes in consumer behavior that will ultimately lead to meaningful and measurable improvements in the environmental aspects of consumer products; 2) to communicate accurate, verifiable, and nondeceptive environmental information to consumers to help them make product choices (in balance with other factors like performance and cost); and 3) to educate consumers about the environmental aspects of products and the role of their purchasing decisions in environmental improvement.

3.2.2 Types of environmental labeling

The term environmental labeling is intended to include all environmental claims associated with products (and in some cases, with services). Three general types of environmental labeling practiced today include third-party seal-of-approval programs, specific claims declarations (either with or without certification), and quantified product environmental information labeling. All of the programs discussed by the workshop participants are voluntary, although some environmental labeling has been made mandatory by government regulations (e.g., energy efficiency labeling, chlorofluorocarbon [CFC] labeling).

Third-party seal-of-approval (seal) programs are designed to identify products or services as being less harmful to the environment as compared to similar products or services with the same function. Specific claims declarations are self-declarations concerning specific attributes of the environmental performance of products. These may be certified by a third party based upon predefined environmental criteria, with the certification appearing on the product label. Quantitative environmental information labeling offers consumers numerical information on the label about a product's environmental performance in multiple categories (e.g., energy consumption, water pollution) without awarding a seal that denotes preferability compared to other products.

Third-party seal-of-approval programs. Currently, all environmental labeling programs that have some type of official governmental sanction are third-party-seal-of-approval programs. These include European Union Eco-labeling Program, the Nordic Countries Program, and the national programs of Canada, France, Germany, the Netherlands, Singapore, New Zealand, and Japan. There are other third-party seal-of-approval programs operated as unofficial labeling programs, such as the Green Seal program in the United States and the Swedish Society for Conservation of Nature program in Sweden. The history and structure of existing environmental labeling programs have been described in detail elsewhere (USEPA 1993). Approximately 12 third-party certification seal-of-approval programs exist worldwide, and several other countries have programs under development (USEPA 1993).

The conceptual process used by most third-party seal-of-approval programs is as follows:
- selection and characterization of a product class for labeling (e.g., interior wall coatings);
- environmental evaluation of the product class;
- identification of most significant environmental impacts and life-cycle stages;

- development of criteria for labeling, including public processes for review and comment; and
- certification and award of seal for product applicants that meet criteria.

Most seal programs attempt to target labeling criteria so that a percentage of the market can meet the criteria as "best in class." A few seal programs sometimes set criteria for environmentally preferable products without regard to whether any products in the marketplace can satisfy the criteria.

Specific claims declarations. Specific claims declarations include familiar single-attribute claims such as "recycled", "biodegradable", "phosphate-free", and "ozone friendly." There are currently two environmental labeling organizations that verify or certify specific single attribute environmental claims made by producers. Scientific Certification Systems (SCS) in the United States not only verifies the specific claims but also permits the use of a seal on a product label with the claims. Green Seal, also in the U.S., verifies specific single-attribute claims, but does not permit the Green Seal logo to appear on the label with the claim.

In the United States, guidelines developed by the Federal Trade Commission (FTC) are intended to discourage deceptive environmental claims by producers. These guidelines discourage the use of general claims, such as "environmentally friendly," and give specific definitions of certain commonly used environmental claims. State attorneys general in the United States have taken action in certain instances to stop the use of deceptive environmental claims, and states now have laws similar to the FTC guidelines. In other nations, claims are governed by "truth in advertising" rules.

Quantitative environmental information labeling. Using a label that profiles a product's environmental information represents a significantly different approach than seal-of-approval type programs or specific claims declaration. Instead of certifying that a product has certain superior environmental attributes as compared to other products in its class based on preset criteria, the environmental information profile approach seeks to convey quantified information about selected environmental attributes of the product to the consumer in a quantitative or qualitative fashion without preset selection criteria or selection of superior products.

At this time, only one private environmental labeling organization in the United States, SCS, offers such a label. It is called an "environmental report card." The purpose of the label is to provide the consumer with the results of a life-cycle inventory of the product bearing the label in an aggregated format using the concept of "environmental burdens." Other similar approaches are under consideration in other countries.

3.3 Status of life-cycle approaches in environmental labeling

3.3.1 Use of life-cycle approaches in third-party seal-of-approval programs

Third-party seal-of-approval programs operate through the development of criteria for product categories. If a product meets the selected criteria, it is eligible for a seal of approval, denoting that the product is environmentally preferable to others in its class. Some of the environmental impacts considered in developing labeling criteria for different products include ozone depletion, global warming, smog formation, human toxicity, noise, energy use, and nonrenewable resource depletion. In most of the product criteria developed to date, only a limited number of aspects of the product's life-cycle environmental impacts are considered after determining in some fashion that these are the most significant attributes that reflect the overall environmental performance of the class of products and can be used to distinguish environmentally superior products. For instance, some criteria for paper products include only the recycled content.

Most third-party seal programs recognize the life-cycle concept in development of labeling criteria for classes of products, but only a few programs use any part of the formal practice of quantitative LCA as it has been defined by the USEPA, SETAC, and others. Where it is used, LCA is being used for two primary purposes: 1) to identify the stages of the life cycle in which the most significant environmental burdens take place, so that labeling criteria can be developed to improve the environmental attributes of these stages; and 2) to identify the most significant types of environmental burdens in those stages and over the life cycle of the product, so that labeling criteria can be developed to address those burdens. LCA does not replace the expert judgment and consensus-building that takes place in the improvement assessment for developing labeling criteria. During this improvement assessment, a whole range of factors comes into play, such as the selection of the most important environmental burdens that drive the criteria, selection of the most effective criteria among several possibilities for improving the overall environmental performance of the product, technical feasibility of meeting the criteria, economic feasibility of meeting the criteria, performance and marketability of products that meet the criteria, and willingness of manufacturers to redesign their products to meet the criteria.

Most of the seal-of-approval programs that have used the formal practice of LCA have used simplified life-cycle inventories with a basic impact analysis. Those who have gone the farthest in the use of formal LCA practices, such as the French, are using the inventory component and elements of impact assessment in classifying and aggregating certain inventory data into global impact indices. The program also relies on certain scoping assumptions to reduce the need for collecting data on every stage of the life cycle for every component of the product. Other programs are utilizing existing LCAs that have been sponsored by manufacturers

CHAPTER 3: ENVIRONMENTAL LABELING   25

or government agencies, and some are using generic LCA databases that have been developed with available data.

The data in Table 3-1 summarize the processes used by several seal programs that are currently operating or have recently operated.

3.3.2 Use of life-cycle approaches in specific claims declarations

Specific claims declarations, whether independently certified or not, are distinguished from other seal-of-approval–type programs in that they focus on only a few specific product environmental attributes, without regard to whether an attribute provides overall environmental benefits or is one of the most significant environmental attributes of the product. For instance, a label certifying that a household cleaner is biodegradable says nothing about whether biodegradability is the most significant indicator of the product's overall environmental impacts or whether the product may have other properties that are significant to the environment.

Specific claims declarations are an important part of environmental labeling because government agencies have been actively encouraging product environmental improvements for certain single attributes through procurement guidelines and market development programs, such as increased use of recycled material and increased energy efficiency. In addition, the FTC and certain state agencies have institutionalized criteria for certain specific environmental claims. Finally, consumers have come to believe that certain environmental attributes of products are relatively beneficial to the environment, and manufacturers are making such claims in order to sell products. Independent certification programs provide the consumer with assurance that the claim has been verified and that the attribute has been measured in some objective fashion by some preset criteria.

A life-cycle approach can be used by companies in several ways to support specific claims, including the following:

- Evaluating the entire life cycle of a product in order to identify those areas where environmental improvements will have the greatest positive effect. This is, for most companies, the primary purpose of LCA. It goes beyond interest in simply supporting external claims to a focus on ensuring that meaningful environmental improvements are made, whether or not the improvements are "marketed" via labeling or advertising.
- Assessing whether a specific environmental claim is derived from a significant phase of a product's life cycle. This use of life-cycle approach is intended only to ensure that the claim is not "trivial" or is not taken from a part of the product's life cycle that is environmentally irrelevant. As a result, it is unusual for the assessment in this case to be based on a fully quantitative LCA; rather, it is based on a qualitative assessment of relevance.

SETAC Press

Table 3-1 Methods used to award

Environmental labeling scheme	Type of approach for criteria development	Decision-making procedure
Australia Environmental Choice	More qualitative Pragmatic method 5 product categories	Steering Committee Scientific Committee defines product criteria Advisory Committee contributes to criteria development, ensures consensus building
Austria	More qualitative with use of few quantitative LCAs 13 product categories	Federal environmental agency proposes product criteria Austrian consumer organization develops criteria through consensus building Ecolabeling committee verifies criteria Ministry of Youth and Family makes final decision Austrian Certification Institute administers label
Canada Environmental Choice	More qualitative life-cycle evaluation, not quantitative LCA 26 product categories	Anyone may propose product criteria Environmental Choice reviews proposal Expert consultant develops technical report in form of briefing note Environmental Choice decides on criteria development and draft criteria Public comments, makes further suggestions (60 days) Environmental Choice makes amendments Ministry of Environment approves final criteria Environmental Choice administers label
France Marque NF Environment (see EU)	Quantitative LCA	Comite de la marque (and advisory scientific council) proposes product Consultant (advisory groups) proposes criteria Comite de la marque reviews/decides on criteria
Germany Blue Angel	More qualitative life-cycle evaluation using matrix Increasingly quantitative 75 product categories	Anyone may propose product Federal environmental agency reviews proposal Environmental label jury selects for criteria development Federal environmental agency develops criteria German institute for quality assurance (RAL) builds consensus Federal environmental agency may revise criteria Environmental label jury reviews/decides on criteria RAL administers label

CHAPTER 3: ENVIRONMENTAL LABELING   27

Table 3-1   continued

Environmental labeling scheme	Type of approach for criteria development	Decision-making procedure
Japan Eco-mark	More qualitative and not life-cycle concept based	Japan Environment Association Promotion Committee proposes and develops criteria in consultation with other committee
	Uses rapidly established, pragmatic criteria	Committee for Approval verifies product eligibility and may require third-party technical verification
	49 product categories	
Nordic Council White Swan Program (Sweden, Norway, Finland, Iceland)	More qualitative life-cycle evaluation plus detailed LCA when necessary and possible	
Netherlands Stichting Milieukeur	More qualitative matrix approach plus use of available quantitative LCAs	Board of experts proposes product criteria
		Consultant recommends criteria
		Board of experts develops criteria through consensus-building
		Public comments, makes further suggestions
		Board of experts reviews/decides on criteria
		Stichting Milieukeur administers label
New Zealand Environmental Choice	Streamlined LCA	Environmental Choice Management Advisory Committee (ECMAC) proposes, draws recommendations concerning products
	Quantitative where deemed necessary and possible	Telarc Council (standards organization) through task groups develops criteria
	9 product categories (end 1992)	ECMAC develops consensus and approves final criteria
United States Green Seal	More qualitative assessment or life-cycle evaluation	Internal evaluation and definition of product criteria through informal contacts
	35 product categories	Draft criteria widely circulated for comments
		Final criteria developed together with document responding to comments
		Verification by Underwriters Laboratories

SETAC Press

Table 3-1 continued

Environmental labeling scheme	Type of approach for criteria development	Decision-making procedure
Denmark (part of EU program)	Quantitative LCA with impact assessment that subdivides into global, regional, and local impacts	
France (part of EU program)	See above - except local manufacturing regulations are excluded in EU program	
Italy (part of EU program)	More qualitative evaluation, not quantitative LCA	
United Kingdom (part of EU program)	More qualitative evaluation, including quantitative evaluation of significant environmental impacts in certain life-cycle stages	

- Supporting a claim might be based on a "holistic" characteristic of the product. In some cases, a specific environmental claim might be based on LCA. This might include, for example, a claim of decreased overall energy use or decreased overall water use. In this case, support for the claim is normally derived from a quantitative life-cycle inventory focused on the particular environmental attribute (e.g., energy, water use), so that all stages of the life cycle are included.

3.3.3 Use of LCA in quantitative environmental information labeling

An example of a quantitative environmental information labeling program is the SCS program, a private environmental labeling organization in the United States. SCS uses an LCA database and model to generate quantitative information on inputs and outputs for the product system. Data are collected directly from the manufacturer of the product and from all stages of the life cycle. Upstream or downstream data may be required to be site-specific or to come from the database, depending upon sensitivity analysis, in order to ensure that the data presented to

SETAC Press

CHAPTER 3: ENVIRONMENTAL LABELING

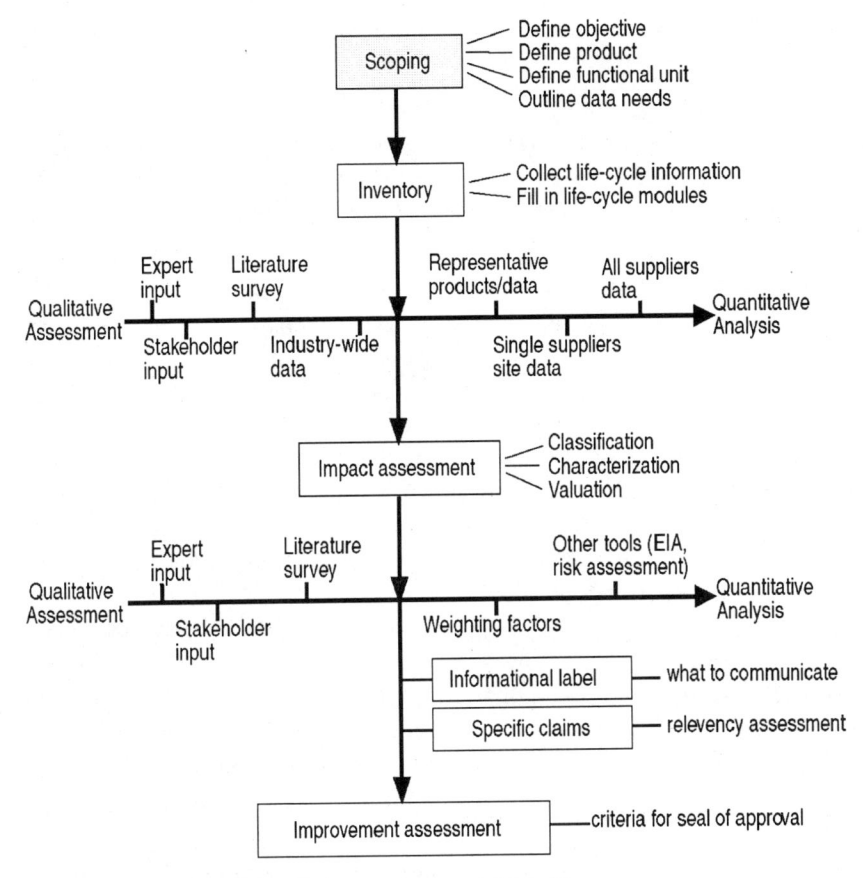

Figure 3-1 Life-cycle approach applied to environmental labeling

the public are representative of that particular product. SCS staff visit manufacturers' facilities to verify data on inputs and outputs and, in some cases, attempt to verify supplier data through contacts with suppliers.

In order to present data from the inventory in a format that will fit on a product label, SCS aggregates the inputs and outputs from the model into categories called environmental burdens. Resource and energy inputs are aggregated based upon chemical or physical properties that can be scientifically identified. Emissions and waste outputs are aggregated based upon government reporting categories under federal environmental regulations in the United States or upon important international treaties such as the Montreal Protocol. Emissions of chemicals that have not been so classified are aggregated and reported as "unclassified" for completeness.

This aggregation of life-cycle inventory (LCI) data into environmental burdens is not intended to be a form of life-cycle impact assessment. In the USEPA and SETAC framework for impact assessment (Fava et al. 1993), the first step is classification of inputs and outputs into impact categories. These impact categories represent a step beyond the Scientific Certification Systems (SCS) environmental burden categories in relating the inputs and outputs to some type of environmental impact. For instance, nitrogen oxides are listed as an SCS environmental burden, but in life-cycle impact assessment, these pollutants would be classified and aggregated with sulfur oxides as acidification emissions or with carbon monoxide and hydrocarbons as smog-forming emissions.

The version of the SCS environmental report card that was launched in August 1993 presents the aggregated environmental burdens as bars on a bar chart. The scale is an exponential scale, so that several orders of magnitude for the different burdens can be represented on the same chart. The label "Better: Lower Burdens" is at the left end of the horizontal bar chart and the label "Worse: Heavier Burdens" is on the right end of the bar chart. The aggregated totals for emissions and other categories are also presented in numerical form.

3.4 Framework for the use of life-cycle approaches in environmental labeling

The use of life-cycle concepts in environmental labeling varies widely in practice, especially with respect to the level of data collection and analysis. These life-cycle approaches, from the more qualitative to the more quantitative, can be described in the general LCA framework. An overall framework of the life-cycle approaches used in environmental labeling programs is shown in Figure 3-1.

In general, all environmental labeling programs conduct some type of "scoping" analysis during the early phases of a project. The purpose of scoping is generally to define the objective of the project, define the product category to be assessed, address issues such as defining functional units and equivalency of use, and generally outline the data that will be needed to conduct the assessment of the environmental attributes of the product or product category to meet the objectives of the study.

The scoping exercise usually results in a proposal for how the assessment will proceed. Scoping is followed by a data collection or "inventory" phase. The purpose of the inventory phase is to collect life-cycle data and other information that "fills in" the life-cycle modules from raw materials extraction to production, use, and ultimate disposal for the product being studied. The level of analysis used in this phase varies along a continuum (Figure 3-1), ranging from a more qualitative approach that tends to rely upon expert judgment, literature searches, and input from stakeholders, to a more quantitative approach that attempts to collect data for each of the modules in a product's life cycle that have been deemed part of the study through the scoping exercise. The output from the inventory phase is nor-

Chapter 3: Environmental Labeling

mally a report on the product's life-cycle burden, expressed either qualitatively, semiquantitatively, or fully quantitatively, as in life-cycle inventory.

Where it is technically feasible and appropriate, the inventory phase is followed by some type of impact assessment. Here, the information from the inventory phase is classified, further characterized, and evaluated, in order to allow identification of the most important characteristics of a product's environmental burden. Like the inventory phase, the impact assessment may vary in its level of detail and collection of data across the qualitative-to-quantitative continuum. Currently, the development of fully quantitative impact assessment is at an early stage, although some quantitative tools for impact assessment are in use. The output from a product impact assessment is normally a prioritized catalog of a product's environmental burdens.

The overall results of the approach from the inventory phase and the impact assessment phase described above are applied to environmental labeling in different ways, depending on the labeling type. In seal-of-approval programs, the results are used to establish seal-award criteria that represent "environmentally preferred" products. For seal programs, another evaluation step is necessary, which is akin to an improvement assessment. The criteria developed through expert judgment and stakeholder input are intended to reduce environmental impacts that are considered the most significant throughout the product's life cycle, with the additional considerations of technical feasibility, cost, performance, and marketability.

In specific environmental claims declarations, the results of the life-cycle approach help establish that a claim is environmentally relevant in the context the product's life cycle. For product information labels, the inventory and the impact assessment results communicate to consumers information on the environmental burdens from the product's life cycle.

3.5 Technical assessment of the application of life-cycle approaches to environmental labeling

3.5.1 Tools for life-cycle approaches in environmental labeling programs

This section describes environmental labeling tools that apply a life-cycle approach. As indicated earlier, environmental labeling programs differ in the extent to which they use different tools in the LCA phases of 1) goal definition and scoping, 2) inventory, and 3) impact assessment. Seal-of-approval labeling programs involve a subsequent step: 4) determination of criteria for identifying environmentally preferable products, which can be considered a form of improvement assessment in LCA terminology.

Background. Environmental labeling programs attempting to assess environmental attributes of products and practitioners performing various phases of life-cycle assessment do not work in a vacuum. Over the years, especially during the last two decades, a body of knowledge has been built to 1) assess and categorize different kinds of environmental and health problems (e.g., acidification, eutrophication, toxicity); 2) determine the pollutants and other environmental stressors that cause or contribute to them; and 3) identify the likely sources of these pollutants and stressors. This background of knowledge contributes information and insights for the scoping and impact assessment phases of life-cycle approaches and has influenced the choice of environmental releases for which data are typically collected in quantitative life-cycle inventories. A host of environmental studies of various kinds, environmental audits and emission data from regulated sources, and ecological and human health risk assessments have contributed, and will continue to contribute, information and insights to be used in life-cycle approaches in environmental labeling and other fields.

Government pollution control programs initially focused on identification of "conventional" pollutants from manufacturing and energy generation processes (e.g., particulates, volatile organic compounds [VOCs], SO_2, NO_x). More recent regulatory requirements have increased the number of toxic pollutants measured and reported by sources. Many government programs require public reporting of industry pollutant release information, thus making this information potentially available for use in environmental labeling programs. Reporting requirements, however, differ substantially from country to country, affecting the nature and quality of information available.

Risk assessments can be generic or more site-specific depending on the manner in which exposure calculations are performed and whether the results are expressed as individual risk or exposed-population risk. Environmental impact assessments (EIAs) are typically site-specific, and numerous EIAs have been performed in the United States for major federal projects and for raw material extraction sites located on federal lands. These typically evaluate a large range of environmental impacts beyond pollutant emissions. This body of information can be utilized to identify types of significant environmental impacts, although great care must be taken when making generalizations based on specific-site information.

The life-cycle approaches used by environmental labeling programs range from the more qualitative to the more quantitative (Figure 3-1). There are tools available throughout the spectrum of approaches.

Tools available for more qualitative approaches. Environmental labeling programs that do not perform quantitative LCA often rely more on expert judgment, literature surveys, stakeholder review, and qualitative evaluation than on collection and evaluation of quantitative data in determining the criteria for labeling. Their approaches take advantage of the store of environmental information dis-

Chapter 3: Environmental Labeling

cussed above. Judgment is required to determine the reliability and pertinence of this information.

Tools available to environmental labeling programs that rely on more qualitative approaches include the following:

- Literature surveys can be used in the scoping, inventory, and impact assessment stages. The literature survey includes a survey of background information (including quantitative information) from environmental impact statements, risk assessments, reports of other tests, and evaluations of pollutants and information in the literature describing various manufacturing processes.

- Expert evaluations are typically performed to profile the market, identify typical components of the product, and assess the environmental attributes of each stage of the life cycle of the product's principal components in a qualitative or semiquantitative manner, based on a literature survey and search for other available information (e.g., from industry). The experts may also propose labeling criteria for consideration. This role may be performed by consultants or by a government agency, often the national environmental agency or a standards-setting institute.

- Checklists or matrices are often used to identify important parts of the life cycle and significant environmental attributes. Generally, consultants or government agency preparers rely on available quantitative information but make a qualitative evaluation based on expert judgment if data are not available in a particular area.

- Expert panels may be convened to review (and possibly supplement) the information and conclusions from the literature survey, the internal expert evaluations, and the checklists/matrices. Panels may include representatives from industry, government agencies, consumer and environmental organizations, scientific organizations, and retailer representatives. Standardization organizations often have a role.

The more qualitative approaches usually incorporate review mechanisms and stakeholder involvement as a way of improving the credibility and acceptance of the results. For example, review boards composed of a broad range of stakeholders are a common feature in environmental labeling programs. Typically, they are used to develop, review, or make final decisions about the criteria for labeling of product categories. Public review and opportunity for public hearing are included in some environmental labeling programs, especially to review the draft labeling criteria.

Table 3-1 describes, in skeletal form, the use of more qualitative approaches in a number of third-party seal-of-approval environmental labeling programs. One example is the Green Seal program, a private environmental labeling organization in the United States, which uses an "environmental impact evaluation" to identify the most significant environmental impacts in each stage of a product's life cycle. Quantitative LCA studies may be used if these are made available by manufacturers, but where these are not available, the product category life cycle is evaluated by reviewing literature and available data from the industry on emissions and other environmental impacts. Advice may be sought from experts in the category from industry and other organizations. Based on the evaluation, key environmental attributes are selected, and criteria representing leadership levels are drafted, aiming to reduce the most significant impacts identified. The criteria are based on expert judgment and attempt to use standard tests and methodologies whenever available. An opportunity for public review and comment is provided, which frequently results in modification of criteria before final adoption.

A more qualitative approach can be used as the life-cycle underpinning for specific claims declarations to determine the overall environmental relevance of the claims being made. Informational labeling, as practiced at present, is quantitative and presupposes a life-cycle inventory.

Tools available for more quantitative approaches. The more quantitative life-cycle approaches for environmental labeling aim toward the quantitative life-cycle assessment methodology that has been described by SETAC and others. They involve considerably more data collection and analysis than the more qualitative approaches.

Some third-party seal-of-approval programs utilize elements of quantitative LCA. In particular, European Union (EU) ecolabeling is moving in this direction. In December 1993, the European Commission set up the Groupe des Sages to advise on the role of LCA in the EU ecolabeling program. The main recommendation of the Groupe des Sages (Udo de Haes 1994), is that quantitative life-cycle assessment can make a significant contribution in providing a scientific, unifying, and transparent basis for the EU program. Figure 3-2 is taken from the Groupe des Sages report and shows the steps in the EU ecolabeling program and how the panel envisions that LCA and its steps can fit into the labeling process.

Currently, the French environmental labeling program is utilizing this approach, both in the French national program and in the EU program. Life-cycle inventory data are collected for the life cycles of actual products that are considered to be representative of the product category in the European market. The inventory results are assessed using the basic life-cycle impact steps of categorization and characterization into impact indices. These data and impact indices serve as the basis for establishing the appropriate criteria for labeling through evaluation by a stakeholder group (e.g., industry, consumers, environmental associations, and government).

By and large, specific claims declarations being used in the marketplace do not rely upon quantitative LCA since they generally do not consider the product's entire life cycle. However, some companies are now internally conducting quan-

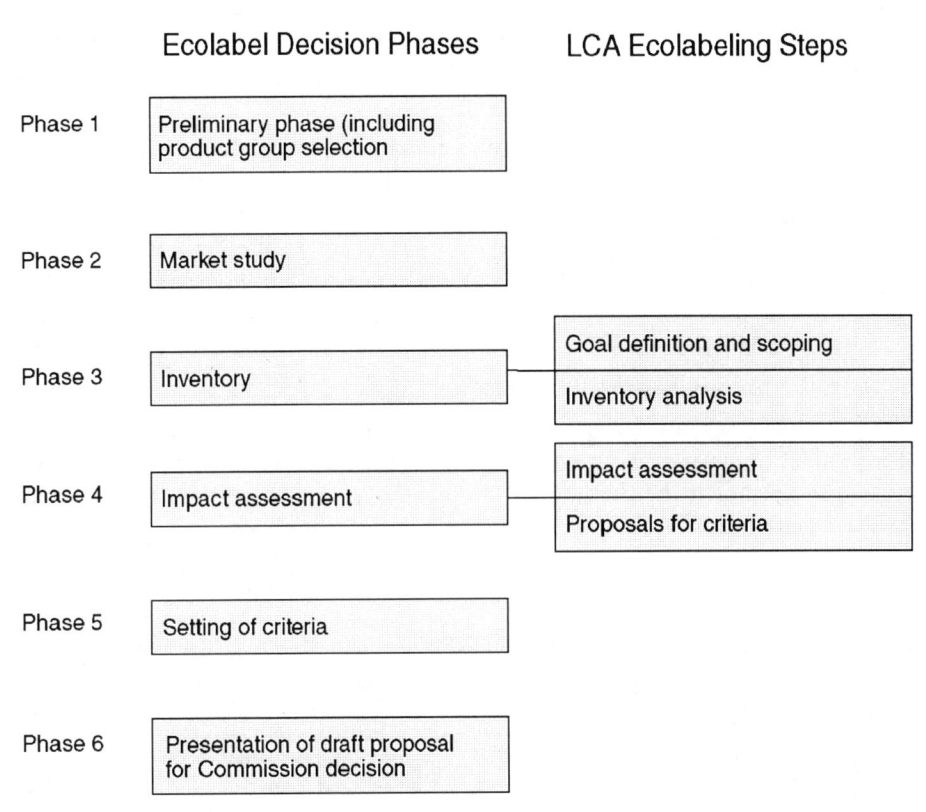

Ecolabel Decision Phases | LCA Ecolabeling Steps

Phase	Ecolabel Decision Phases	LCA Ecolabeling Steps
Phase 1	Preliminary phase (including product group selection	
Phase 2	Market study	
Phase 3	Inventory	Goal definition and scoping / Inventory analysis
Phase 4	Impact assessment	Impact assessment / Proposals for criteria
Phase 5	Setting of criteria	
Phase 6	Presentation of draft proposal for Commission decision	

Figure 3-2   European Union ecolabeling and LCA steps

titative LCAs to support and verify specific declared claims. In some cases, third-party certification of these claims is utilized.

Quantified product information labeling currently utilizes quantitative LCA. In determining the critical indices to be displayed, this program emphasizes both site-specific data collection and the use of existing LCA databases to produce an environmental profile for a particular product.

3.5.2 Technical issues in quantitative LCA in environmental labeling

Goal, scoping, and definition. An ecolabeling program is inherently a comparison of products that perform the same function in the marketplace. Therefore, functionality, functional unit, and equivalency of use are key factors in the initial phases of an LCA approach to environmental labeling. All the performance characteristics of a product for a given functionality (e.g., in the case of interior paints, coverage, and film durability) should be factored into performance equivalency. One method for determining the proper functional unit is to perform a market survey, identifying products that perform similar functions and their key performance attributes.

Life-cycle inventory. The inventory component of an LCA should be conducted with a sufficient number of representative products to support the environmental claim/label.

In the case of third-party seal-of-approval programs, the products selected should be representative of the market. A full LCA inventory could be performed on this representative sample of products to determine the range of LCA inventory data needed to establish a significant range of differences in the category. From this analysis, the range of data can form the basis for judging environmental preferability. A full life-cycle inventory could be performed on these representative products to highlight the main environmental burdens associated with this category of products during their life cycle.

Specific declared claims programs depend on validating a specific characteristic of a product at a particular stage of its life cycle. Life-cycle inventory data could be used to document the claim. For example, in the claim of eliminating cadmium (heavy metal) from an electrical switch, a life-cycle inventory revealed that cadmium was used in large amounts in the upstream manufacturing process; therefore, in this case, the claim was demonstrated to be invalid.

Quantified product information label programs, as currently practiced, have a complete life-cycle inventory for the product and for ancillary materials, including all packaging.

Data quality. The quality of data must be sufficiently accurate to support the environmental label (EL)/claim being made. Types and sources of data should be identified, with the exception of confidential, business, and patent information. The key role of practitioners is to ensure the quality of the data, while protecting the confidentiality interests of industry.

Data maintenance should be sufficient to support the claim program made in the marketplace. Traditional LCAs are snapshots; thus, to the extent that technologies change, EL/claims should be regularly revised and updated.

Impact assessment. There should be sufficient impact assessment techniques applied to the inventory to support the EL/claims being made, recognizing that there are currently limitations in the methodology.
- Classification: Third-party seal-of-approval programs and quantified product information label programs can reduce inventory data through classification and partitioning techniques.
- Characterization: Third-party seal-of-approval programs and quantified product information label programs may utilize limited characterization techniques to further relate inventory data to known environmental indices (e.g., ozone depletion index). Environmental impacts at various geographical scales should be addressed, from global (climate change) to local (noise, water effluent, occupational health).

CHAPTER 3: ENVIRONMENTAL LABELING

- Valuation: Classification and characterization techniques should be used as far as technically feasible to maintain the objectivity of the overall impact assessment. Only after classification and characterization, a valuation phase should be applied with great care and transparency. In the case of third-party seal-of-approval programs, choices should be made by a group of stakeholders in an iterative consensus process, in order to determine the appropriate criteria and thresholds (e.g., hurdles) for awarding the label. A representative stakeholder group (e.g., industry, consumers, environmental associations, and government) should be involved in this determination of criteria, to ensure that the environmental priorities reflect the societal values.

For specified declared claims, valuation techniques have not been commonly used but should be seriously considered for application in a similar manner to seal-of-approval programs.

In the case of quantified product information label programs, choices should be made by a group of stakeholders in an iterative consensus process, in order to determine the appropriate indices and units to be displayed on the label.

3.5.3 Strengths and weaknesses of more qualitative versus more quantitative approaches in environmental labeling

More qualitative life-cycle approaches. Strengths of more qualitative life-cycle approaches include these
- Less time and fewer resources are needed to perform the evaluation.
- Less time and fewer resource needs mean that more products can be evaluated and labeled.
- Expert evaluation of the most significant environmental impacts early in the process allows more time for detailed evaluation of those impacts.
- Collection of potentially unnecessary data to fill in all of the life-cycle matrix is avoided.

Weaknesses of more qualitative life-cycle approaches include these:
- The lack of quantitative inventory data increases the degree of uncertainty about conclusions drawn from the evaluation.
- This uncertainty grows with more complex product categories and for functions that can be performed by several very different types of products.
- Impact assessment using qualitative information is not a fully developed or agreed-upon methodology.
- The use of expert judgments instead of the LCA inventory approach in some cases is more subject to questions about credibility, unless there is a peer review process concerning those judgments.

More quantitative approaches. Strengths of more quantitative approaches include these

- A quantified measure of functionality and use equivalency is used as the basis for the evaluation, allowing for a more fair comparison of different products.
- Trade-offs among environmental impacts are more explicitly identified.
- A more detailed look at a product's materials and processes provides manufacturers a basis for measuring continuous improvement outside the context of the labeling program.
- Life-cycle inventory data facilitates the selection of quantitative criteria for labeling that can be focused more on environmental performance and less on lists of "good" and "bad" ingredients.

Weaknesses of more-quantitative life-cycle approaches include these:

- Quantitative LCA is resource and time-intensive, especially when categories of products are examined.
- The more complex the product category and/or its function being studied, the higher the level of uncertainty; and the more data required to overcome uncertainties.
- Data availability and quality presently limit the types of product categories that can be covered.
- Quantitative results do not always mean more accurate results because they may mask assumptions and judgment made during the analyses, unless such decisions are transparent.
- LCA methodology is not fully developed because quantitative impact assessment is not yet fully developed and agreed upon.

3.6 Measuring the effectiveness of life-cycle approaches in ecolabeling programs

The purpose of the following section is to describe ways of assessing the value of life-cycle approaches in environmental labeling programs. To do so naturally requires considering the overall purpose of environmental labeling and how the effectiveness of these programs may be measured. Measuring the overall effectiveness of environmental labeling programs, however, has been a difficult and controversial task. To date, no assessment has been made of the overall impact environmental labeling programs have had, either on the marketplace or on environmental improvement. Consequently, this section will focus on how life-cycle approaches may be used to advance the stated objectives of environmental labeling programs.

3.6.1 Why measure?
In order to effectively gauge the utility of quantitative or qualitative life-cycle approaches in environmental labeling programs, some form of performance measurement will be required. This will allow public policy stakeholders to assess
- the degree to which life-cycle approaches are being utilized within labeling programs;
- the extent to which labeling programs are using more qualitative versus more quantitative life-cycle approaches;
- if and how the chosen life-cycle approach has contributed to the effectiveness of labeling programs;
- how the chosen life-cycle approach supports, or is supported by, other decision-making tools used by labeling programs; and
- how effectively the results of the life-cycle approach used are being communicated by labeling programs.

Given that environmental labeling programs have made more use of life-cycle concepts than other public policy tools, performance reviews may also contribute significantly to the resolution of many of the technical issues involved in the use of life-cycle approaches in other public policy settings. An additional benefit from performance measurement will be a review of the life-cycle data generated by labeling programs, which may contribute to the overall body of life-cycle information available for public policy use.

3.6.2 Who measures?
A number of options exist with respect to who would be responsible for performance reviews:
- independent peer review committees consisting of representative stakeholders could be established;
- labeling programs could establish their own review process and make the results of this review available to interested stakeholders; or
- national governments and/or international organizations such as OECD, ISO (International Standard Organization) or UNEP (United National Environment Program) could conduct such reviews.

3.6.3 What should be measured: specific issues to address in a performance review
The following are specific issues that could be addressed in evaluating the use of life-cycle approaches in environmental labeling:
- Is the chosen life-cycle approach, either qualitative or quantitative, accurately described and communicated by the program to all stakeholders? For example, if a program states that it has used a fully quantitative LCA methodology, has it conducted an inventory plus impact assessment or only an inventory? Alternatively, if a qualitative approach, such as an

expert decision matrix, has been used, has this process and its limitations been communicated accurately and transparently?
- Has the chosen life-cycle approach contributed to the overall goal of continual environmental improvement of the industries within the product categories considered?
- Has the chosen life-cycle approach helped identify with greater accuracy the key environmental attributes for consideration?
- Has the chosen life-cycle approach enhanced consumer acceptance of the environmental labeling program or enhanced the changes in the marketplace intended by the labeling program?
- Has the chosen life-cycle approach enhanced the scientific credibility of the environmental labeling program?
- Has the chosen life-cycle approach resulted in better decisions from the standpoint of overall environmental improvements of the products being labeled?
- Has the chosen life-cycle approach enhanced transparency of value judgments used in the labeling process?
- To the extent that the performance review compares the use of life-cycle approaches in different labeling programs, what is the level of consistency in the application of the tools from product category to product category?
- If an impact assessment phase has been carried out, has it used a prevailing, scientifically based methodology? If not, are modifications or judgments sufficiently explained and justified?
- Have the costs of more quantitative life-cycle approaches limited access by some segments of industry to the labeling program?

3.6.4 Timing of the performance review

The frequency of conducting performance reviews will be dictated to some extent by the degree to which LCA is being adopted by the labeling community (either conceptual or quantitative), the actual number LCAs being conducted, and who is performing the review.

3.7 Stakeholder involvement in the use of life-cycle approaches in environmental labeling

This section addresses the involvement of stakeholders in the process of environmental labeling and the extent to which the use of life-cycle approaches influences or necessitates their involvement.

Most third-party certification seal-of-approval environmental labeling programs involve multiple stakeholders in the process of developing the criteria for labeling. Some work on a public-notice-and-comment model, while others involve multi-stakeholder committees in making decisions on labeling criteria. In addition, most programs rely heavily upon producers for information in the environmental evaluation of product categories.

In the public-notice-and-comment model, the environmental evaluation of the product category and the draft labeling criteria developed from that evaluation are performed internally or by consultants. Draft criteria are then provided to interested stakeholders during a comment period, and meetings may be held with key stakeholder groups. Stakeholders include producers, government agencies, and environmental and consumer groups. Comments are then considered in revising the draft labeling criteria and producing the final criteria for certification.

In the multi-stakeholder committee model, either a permanent representative committee is created to oversee all product criteria or ad hoc committees are convened to determine criteria for particular product categories. The environmental evaluation provides the input to the committee for the determination of labeling criteria. Committees often include representatives of industry, environmental and consumer organizations, government agencies, and trade unions. In many programs using this model, the criteria are actually determined by the committee, while in others, the committee approves or disapproves draft criteria developed by the staff of the labeling organization. Further, public input may be sought after the committee determines the criteria and before a final decision is made; in some cases, government approval is required.

Specific claims declarations involve only the producer, and in some instances, a verification organization, in the process of evaluating the claim. Quantified environmental information labeling involves both the producer and the labeling organization in developing the information for the label and can also include some type of peer review for the life-cycle study performed.

Because of the potential for misuse, labeling or environmental claims that are based on an LCA of a product or service, or that imply that the product or service is environmentally preferable overall, should use some form of multi-stakeholder peer review for the underlying life-cycle study. The SETAC Guidelines for Life-Cycle Assessment (Consoli et al. 1993) recommend that LCA studies intended for public audiences (e.g., through labeling) utilize an interactive, multi-stakeholder, peer-review process. There is no reason to distinguish quantitative LCA studies from other life-cycle approaches in the need for some type of peer review where environmental claims based on the life cycle are made. For third-party seal programs, this peer review may occur through the public-notice-and-comment model or the multi-stakeholder committee model.

3.8 Communication of life-cycle approaches used in environmental labeling programs

As stated in the SETAC Guidelines for Life-Cycle Assessment: A "Code of Practice" (Consoli et al. 1993), presentation and communication are a vital element of any LCA. The "code of practice" recognizes that objective and transparent reporting of results is crucial to improving environmental performance. This principle is magnified in environmental labeling programs that utilize LCA to influence consumer behavior as well as to stimulate environmental improvement by industry. This principle is equally important for environmental labeling programs that rely upon more qualitative life-cycle approaches.

Issues related to the most appropriate way for a label to communicate environmental claims (e.g., seal-of-approval vs. informational labels) were considered beyond the scope of this workshop. From a public policy perspective, however, there are a number of issues of importance including

- whether the label portrays life-cycle information in a way that is not misleading;
- whether and how underlying life-cycle studies that support the labeling program are available to stakeholders;
- whether life-cycle information is accurately portrayed to public audiences who are not familiar with the complexity of the methodologies used; and
- the extent to which the chosen life-cycle approach (quantitative versus qualitative) affects the accuracy and scope of claims made by ecolabeling programs.

3.8.1 Generic communications requirements

The label itself does not need to communicate whether or not a quantitative LCA was done. The important requirement is that the life-cycle information underlying the label be available to stakeholders in some manner. The type of information and the transparency of that information should follow the SETAC Guidelines for Life-Cycle Assessment: A "Code of Practice" (Consoli et al. 1993), taking into account the level of data and analysis involved. Specific requirements identified by the "Code of Practice" for LCA reports include information on the objectives of the study, the scope of the study, system boundaries, flow diagrams, detailed methodology, data sources and presentation, conclusions and summary report, peer review, and practitioner qualifications. These reports should be made available on request to all interested stakeholders.

The remainder of the discussion will focus on issues related to different types of labeling programs.

3.8.2 Third-party seal-of-approval programs

In seal-of-approval programs, the labeling authority may use both quantitative and qualitative life-cycle information in the criteria-setting process. The consumer is not the direct recipient of the life-cycle information and, as such, has no first-hand information about the life-cycle data used to award the seal. In this case, it is important for the labeling authority to make an evaluation report available to stakeholders, including marketers, producers, consumers, government agencies, and environmental organizations with an interest in the labeling program. The report should clearly describe the approach that was used to develop the criteria and should clearly communicate the degree to which more quantitative versus more qualitative life-cycle approaches were used.

3.8.3 Specific claims declarations

Self-declared claims are normally focused on single attributes and in most cases do not utilize life-cycle approaches in the development of the claim. In rare cases where a self-declared claim indicates that a life-cycle study has been used to substantiate the claim, the nonproprietary results of that study should be made available to interested stakeholders.

3.8.4 Quantified product information labels

In the case of currently available quantified product information labels, life-cycle information is provided directly to the consumer. Since quantified product information labels are based on quantified LCA studies, the above-mentioned SETAC guidelines would apply directly to this type of program.

3.9 Conclusions and recommendations

Environmental labeling, and particularly third-party seal-of-approval labeling, is one current use of the life-cycle concept in public policy. Practically all third-party seal programs at least consider the life-cycle concept in their selection of criteria for labeling eligibility. Some environmental labeling programs utilize elements of quantitative LCA in their development of criteria for product labeling, and the EU ecolabeling program has embarked upon the development of guidelines for the use of quantitative life-cycle assessment.

While a fully quantitative life-cycle approach is not a prerequisite for environmental labeling, in order for environmental labeling programs to truly address the overall environmental burdens of products, they all should use a life-cycle approach. It is recognized that certain specific environmental claims may be made because government regulations or public perceptions deem certain product attributes to be significant enough to communicate to consumers, independent of life-cycle considerations. Communications based on such regulations and perceptions should also be reviewed from the perspective of the life-cycle concept to ensure that the specific communications required (e.g., recycled content) are significant in the overall environmental burdens of a product system.

SETAC Press

In using life-cycle approaches, environmental labeling programs should focus on collecting sufficient data and information on a product's life cycle to ensure that the end result of labeling is technically defensible, accurate, verifiable, and nondeceptive. In particular, labeling programs should achieve the following:

- For seal-of-approval programs, the level of data collected and the analysis conducted should be sufficient to ensure that the chosen criteria provide a sufficient basis for determining that specific products are meaningfully declared "environmentally preferred" compared to others in the same product category.
- For specific environmental claims, the level of data collected and the analysis conducted should ensure that the attribute being communicated is environmentally relevant in the context of the product's life cycle.
- For product information programs, the level of data collected and the analysis conducted should be sufficient to ensure that meaningful and environmentally relevant information about the life cycle is provided to the consumer.

Because of the potential for misuse, labeling or environmental claims that are based on the life cycle of a product or service or that imply that the product or service is environmentally preferable overall, should use some form of multi-stakeholder peer review for the underlying life-cycle study. This can include public-notice-and-comment approaches as well as ad hoc and permanent expert review groups. Peer review should be included for both those programs that use more qualitative approaches as well as for those that use more quantitative approaches.

An environmental label itself does not need to communicate the extent to which a quantitative LCA was done. The important requirement is that the life-cycle information underlying the label be available to stakeholders in some manner. The type of information and the transparency of that information should follow the SETAC Guidelines for Life-Cycle Assessment: "A Code of Practice" (Consoli et al. 1993), taking into account the level of data and analysis involved.

3.10 References

Consoli F, Allen D, Boustead I, Fava J, Franklin W, Jensen A, de Oude N, Parrish R, Perriman R, Postlethwaite D, Quay B, Séguin J, Vigon B, editors. 1993. Guidelines for life-cycle assessment: a "code of practice." Society of Environmental Toxicology and Chemistry (SETAC) and SETAC-Europe Workshop; 1993 Mar; Sesimbra Portugal. Pensacola FL: SETAC Pr.

Fava J, Consoli F, Denison R, Dickson K, Mohin T, and Vigen B, editors. 1993. Conceptual framework for impact assessment. Society of Environmental Toxicology and Chemistry (SETAC) Pellston Workshop; 1992 Feb 1-6; Sandestin FL. Pensacola FL: Setac Pr.

Udo de Haes HA, chairman. 1994. Guidelines for the application of life-cycle assessment in the EU ecolabelling programme. Groupe des Sages, First Report, May 1994. Leiden, the Netherlands.

[USEPA] U.S. Environmental Protection Agency. 1993. The use of life-cycle assessment in labeling programs, Office of Pollution Prevention and Toxics. EPA/742-R-93-003.

Chapter 4
Acquisition and Procurement

4.1 Introduction

4.1.1 Scope
This chapter considers the role of the life-cycle concepts in the acquisition and procurement of systems, products and supplies, services, technologies, facilities, and other commercially acquired items and activities (collectively referred to as products in the remainder of this chapter). In general, the broader the scope of the acquired product, the greater the need for and the more complex the task of applying life-cycle thinking to evaluate environmental features of product performance.

The chapter is organized into several major sections. In Section 4.2, the general concepts associated with applying life-cycle concepts to acquisition and procurement decisions are defined. These general concepts and principles are illustrated with case studies on acquisition decisions in Section 4.3. Procurement issues and case studies are presented in Section 4.4. Section 4.5 describes a set of life-cycle tools that have relevance to acquisition and procurement. Sections 4.6 and 4.7 address implementation issues and provide a set of recommendations. Section 4.8 describes future needs.

The material presented in this chapter will focus primarily on government acquisition and procurement activities; however, the applicability and use of the life-cycle concepts described in this chapter potentially pertain to all acquisition and procurement processes in both the public and private sectors.

4.1.2 Definitions
In addition to the definitions commonly used throughout this document, this section develops two additional terms important to this chapter:

Acquisition is a process that begins with definition of the user's needs, continues through creation of the desired product (via research, design, development, test, and evaluation), comes to fruition through construction or production of the product, and concludes with its final decommissioning or disposal. Two key elements are these: 1) there is an opportunity to include features that deliver specific performance in creation of the product and 2) large acquisitions entail scope and resource expenditures of a magnitude that make it worthwhile to undertake evaluative processes that are highly tailored and data intensive.

Procurement is a subset of acquisition, generally dealing with products that already exist or require only modest modifications to meet user requirements. Unlike acquisition, procurement offers less opportunity to have a significant effect on performance characteristics of any of the alternative products.

4.1.3 Environmental considerations in the acquisition process

Although the USEPA, as well as state and local environmental agencies, are primarily responsible for protecting the nation's land, water, and air, there is an increased recognition that government can make a contribution in protecting the environment through its role as both a supplier and consumer of goods and services. This chapter focuses on how government (primarily the federal government), as a consumer, can take a leadership role in continuous environmental improvement and how life-cycle concepts can facilitate this goal. This chapter is written from the perspective of the federal government, but other levels of government play a similar role and it is hoped that they may also benefit from the discussions and examples in this chapter.

Traditionally, the goal of an acquisition program is to deliver to the user a product that provides acceptable performance (e.g., speed, endurance, capacity, reliability, maintainability), on schedule, and at a reasonable cost (e.g., financial managers typically evaluate peak annual outlays, total cost over the life cycle, and unit cost).

The goal of applying life-cycle concepts in an acquisition program is to determine the environmental features of the program. This will allow an agency to identify and address environmental issues by changes in product design, development, test procedures, material choices, manufacturing processes, operating and support processes, and decommissioning and disposal processes.

4.1.4 Stakeholders

Previous SETAC and USEPA documents on LCA have stressed the need to involve appropriate stakeholders in all phases of LCA design and execution (Consoli et al. 1993). The choice of these stakeholders depends upon the purposes and audience of the particular LCA. For LCA applications that guide product improvement, for example, the selection of stakeholders is entirely at the discretion of the officials involved in the decision. In contrast, LCAs for external (*e.g.* marketing claims) or public purposes require the involvement of a far broader range of stakeholders.

The definition of stakeholders for acquisitions and procurement by public agencies raises issues that do not necessarily arise in other life-cycle contexts. Unlike private firms making purchases, public agencies retain strict accountability to a broad range of stakeholders. Unlike other public life-cycle applications, however, these external stakeholders have historically had a more limited role in the acquisition and procurement process. Thus, for example, a new regulation requires open notification and the collection of and response to public comment, with no qualifications upon the commenting public. Procurement contracts, in contrast, are generally required to be open to all potential suppliers but have little or no provision for participation by other potential stakeholders.

4.1.5 The role of life-cycle concepts in acquisition and procurement

Within the acquisition and procurement process, life-cycle concepts can play an important and synergistic role with existing processes. Fundamentally, every acquisition or procurement process is designed to provide the best value for the task at hand. Tradition-

CHAPTER 4: ACQUISITION AND PROCUREMENT   49

ally, acquisition and procurement processes balance the performance attributes of products against other factors such as cost, quality, and service (see Figure 4-1). Including environmental elements in acquisition and procurement processes requires the addition of environmental criteria in this fundamental value equation, elevating environmental considerations to the same plane as other considerations (see Figure 4-2).

Life-cycle concepts can help to determine where the most appropriate and effective intervention in the acquisition and procurement process should occur. In addition, life-cycle concepts can help to identify what tools should be used to best integrate environmental considerations into the acquisition and procurement process. Finally, the combination of effective use of life-cycle concepts and the appropriate use of assessment tools can help to define the environmental impacts associated with acquisition and procurement decisions.

In practice, life-cycle concepts help to
1) identify points in the product development cycle where environmentally significant decisions can be made,
2) integrate environmental information into those decisions, and
3) identify alternatives that provide decreased environmental burdens.

Life-cycle concepts or their constituent tools do not make the final decisions. Rather, life-cycle concepts in the acquisition and procurement process can provide additional input to decision-makers, helping them include environmental considerations in their decisions.

4.2 General concepts and issues
A number of issues germane to both acquisition and procurement processes and their use of life-cycle concepts have been identified and are discussed in this section.

4.2.1 Who is a stakeholder?
The use of life-cycle concepts in the acquisition/procurement process, as described in the introduction, can be seen as having to address two quite distinct visions of stakeholder involvement: the broad view proposed by the life-cycle community and the more limited vision embodied in historical public policy processes.

Further, in the government acquisitions process, and to a more limited extent in procurement, there may be multiple stakeholders within the government, either within a single agency or distributed across multiple agencies involved in the acquisition process. Any effort to broaden the scope of stakeholder involvement to include new parties (such as environmental advocacy groups) will need to address the institutional concerns and historical perspectives of these traditional stakeholder groups.

For example, the process for major systems acquisition in the federal government that has developed over several decades includes the following internal stakeholders:
1) the user who defined the need for the acquisition and will use the final product;

SETAC Press

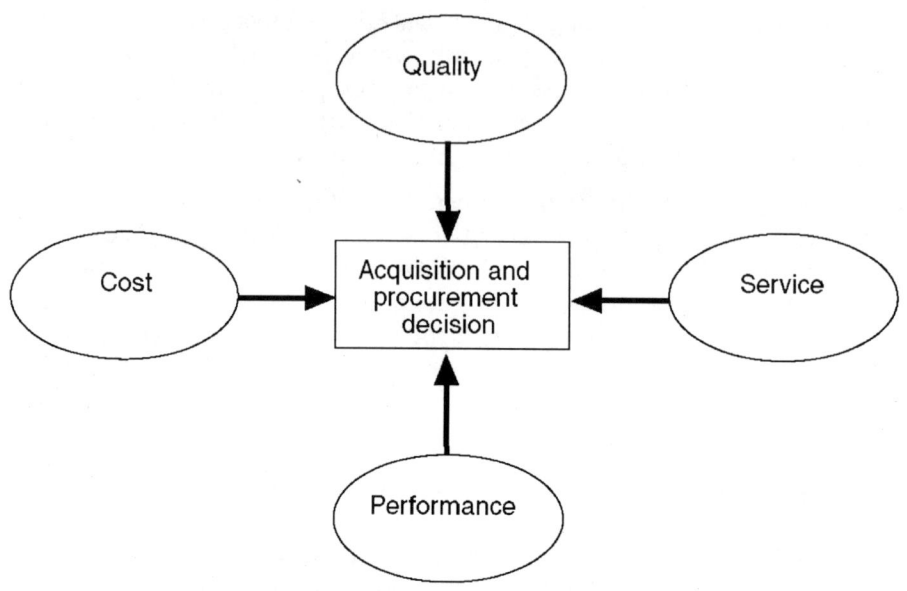

Figure 4-1   Traditional approach: acquisition and procurement decision

2) program managers, systems engineers, and their contractors, who design, develop, and manufacture the product;
3) an independent test community that demonstrates product effectiveness;
4) financial managers who provide resources and oversee their expenditure; and
5) functional staffs to ensure that the product is reliable, maintainable, and supportable by logistics staffs.

Among the additional stakeholders who potentially could be involved in the application of life-cycle concepts in the acquisition/procurement process are the following groups:
- the agency making the acquisition/procurement
- oversight agencies in the same or different branches of government
- the agency for which the acquisition/procurement was made (if different from the agency making the acquisition/procurement, as in the case of the General Services Administration)
- potential vendors/contractors for the specified technology type
- small business representatives
- potential vendors/contractors for alternative technologies or products
- trade associations
- advocacy groups concerned with fiscal responsibility
- environmental advocacy groups
- taxpayers and/or the general public

Chapter 4: Acquisition and Procurement

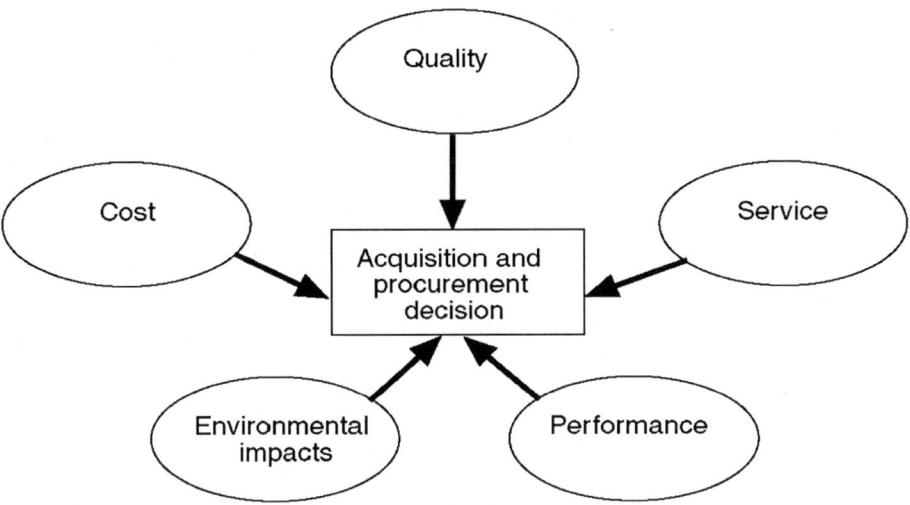

Figure 4-2   Strategic approach: acquisition and procurement decision

4.2.2 Consensus

Consensus plays an important role in LCA and other life-cycle approaches. It is reflected in efforts to involve all relevant stakeholders in decisions, in peer review of studies, and even in the processes used to develop underlying scientific documents by SETAC and others.

Many public policy decisions, in contrast, are not based upon achieving consensus. Rather, the standard for much of public policy-making is that all stakeholders have an opportunity for input. In some cases, there is also an explicit requirement that the decision-maker formally respond to (if only to reject) such input. In the area of acquisition and procurement, outside input may be even more limited. In many cases, the only real external requirement is to ensure that all potential suppliers have equal access for bidding purposes.

The attempt to integrate a process that has operated on consensus principles into processes that are adversarial or even litigious (at least as far as external stakeholders are concerned) would seem to call for adjustment in one or the other. While an argument could be made for changing the American public policy process to a consensus mode, it seems somewhat more realistic to address the issue of how to develop life-cycle methodologies that are applicable in processes with a complete or near-complete absence of consensus.

Among the issues that must be considered in integrating life-cycle concepts into the acquisition and procurement process are these:

- Is consensus necessary anywhere in the process? If so, where and among what group of stakeholders? By what authority (professional, administrative, etc.) do these stakeholders impose their consensus-based decisions on other stakeholders?

SETAC Press

- Can life-cycle procedures effectively be adapted to a non-consensus process and still retain effective stakeholder involvement? How?
- How is the concept of peer review related to the public notification and comment process? Can procedures to implement the one be adapted to serve the other? Is either suitable to the acquisition and procurement process?
- Can consensus serve as a surrogate for objectivity, insulating the acquisition and procurement authority from charges of arbitrariness?

4.2.3 Valuation

In the practice of LCA, critical importance has been placed on making any incorporated value judgments, as well as scientific and technical assumptions, "transparent." In other words, anyone presented with a life-cycle study should be able to clearly identify any and all value judgments that it contains.

Moreover, the LCA process described in SETAC (Consoli et al. 1993) and USEPA (1994) documents explicitly defers valuation of different environmental impacts to the end of the life-cycle impact assessment, in order both to distinguish it from the relatively more technical aspects of inventory and impact assessment and to ensure that alternative stakeholders can apply their own values to the results of the inventory, classification, and categorization efforts. The central concept has been that LCA is one of several tools to aid in making decisions, but that a single life-cycle process can yield a variety of different decisions, depending upon stakeholder values. There is no single "right" answer.

The parties who will be involved in valuation (stakeholders) are assumed to vary according to the intended application of the life-cycle study. Thus, for purely internal studies, the conducting organization is presumed to be entirely free to apply its own value system (e.g., return on investment). For externally used studies, current codes of LCA practice recommend the explicit inclusion of a broader stakeholder group.

This general conceptual approach to valuation has a number of advantages. It provides a mechanism for stakeholder groups with differing values to share a common analytical framework and to avoid commingling technical (and presumably resolvable) differences in viewpoint with more fundamental philosophical disagreements that are beyond the scope of technical calculations. It also allows the life-cycle practitioner to be removed from the more contentious realms of environmental and social policy and to assume the professional distance of the "technologist."

It may well be, however, that this conceptualization of the valuation process is too narrow to accurately reflect real markets and acquisition and procurement processes. While conceptually, a practitioner may present a decision-maker with neutral information to which the decision-maker can apply a value system, in reality the practitioner will always be limited to presenting a very restricted subset of the potentially relevant information. In many cases (e.g., labeling of consumer products), the restriction of the information to be presented is severe.

SETAC Press

The need to select the information that is presented inherently means that the presentation of information to a decision-maker itself entails valuation. This is not limited to the more egregious instances of selective LCA reporting that have been documented but also applies to any reporting of product attributes, regardless of whether they can be objectively verified. For example, the simple information that a product contains some percentage of recycled material inherently asserts the value judgment that recycled content reflects a significant environmental characteristic of the product and that the product is preferable to one with a lesser recycled content. For any given product, this may or may not be true.

Those seeking to incorporate life-cycle concepts into acquisition and procurement decisions must deal with such selective reporting of information, whether they are relying on information developed by external sources (potential suppliers or third-party certification organizations) or synthesizing information for their own management and stakeholders. Explicit standards or procedures for distinguishing appropriate and inappropriate selection of reported information may need to be developed.

As noted earlier, the life-cycle framework that has been developed thus far assigns valuation to the stakeholder. The corresponding standard assumption in discussions of life-cycle applications in the marketplace is that the customer will apply values to the determination of what is environmentally preferable. Thus, while labeling organizations, for example, have an obligation to present information that is known to them regarding the environmental significance of the measurements and claims that they report, and to ensure that in their judgment the reported information addresses the most important environmental characteristics of the product, the ultimate application of environmental values to the reported information rests with the purchaser.

4.2.4 The unique nature of the customer in public procurement

In the area of government procurement, the distinction between analyst and customer blurs. The procuring agency automatically assumes the role both of analyst and customer. While conceivably the former role could be assigned to another party (a contractor or third-party certification organization), the latter role, and its requirement to assign values to environmental outcomes, cannot be avoided. Further, unlike the private individual or corporate customer, the public agency has an obligation to avoid arbitrary decisions and to be responsive to the values of the public. Although this conceptual framework is likely to be modified in the face of initiatives to "reinvent" government and bring it more into conformity with standard business practices, the need to act as a responsible agent for external stakeholders will remain.

As a customer organization becomes accountable to a broadening range of external or internal stakeholders, its obligations for openness and consensus in setting criteria and making decisions increase. This expectation, however, does entail an increased risk of procedural burdens and delays involved in completing an acquisition or procurement. This is of particular concern for governmental customers, which answer to a range of public entities.

SETAC Press

4.2.5 Interdependence of stakeholders, consensus, and valuation

The preceding discussion has addressed the issues of stakeholder identification, consensus-building, and valuation as if they were independent processes. In reality, they are heavily interdependent. The selection of stakeholders will influence the likelihood of obtaining consensus with respect to valuation and will change the distribution of value systems that must be represented in the consensus process. The process used to develop consensus can affect the willingness of different stakeholder groups to participate, as will the choice of metrics to be employed for valuation. The valuation metrics will condition the consensus process, which in turn can affect the ultimate valuation.

The success of this entire process will ultimately depend on the extent to which the selected stakeholders for the valuation exercise mirror the stakeholder communities in the real world. This is likely to require a process of continuing improvement, as new stakeholder communities react to the results of valuation and consensus-building efforts.

4.2.6 Win-win opportunities

While it may not be possible to avoid producing winners and losers through the use of life-cycle concepts in acquisition and procurement, the broadest possible success from deploying these processes can be achieved by maximizing the number of stakeholder winners, in particular the following:

- Agencies and program managers are winners when they are able to meet their other acquisition requirements while implementing an environmentally preferable product program.
- Acquisition and procurement personnel are winners when they are able to make sound, knowledgeable purchasing decisions and are recognized for doing so.
- Suppliers and contractors are winners when they have an open and equal opportunity to participate in the process and when they are not unfairly excluded or disadvantaged due to arbitrary, non-objective definitions or determinations of environmental preferability.
- Government environmental agencies are winners when they develop and provide sound, objective guidance that allows best-available environmentally preferable acquisition and procurement decision-making and that minimizes agency and procurement exposure to charges of unfair or unlawful practices relating to environmentally preferable acquisition and procurement. One way to minimize this potential exposure to stakeholder criticism or challenge is through the development of consensus-based environmental criteria, performance, or standards.
- State and local government procurement officials are winners if federal practices afford exemplary benchmarks to be used at the state and local levels.
- Environmental and other nongovernmental organizations are winners when continuous environmental improvement is achieved through environmentally preferable acquisition and procurement activities.

Chapter 4: Acquisition and Procurement

- Citizens and taxpayers are winners if acquisition and procurement practices lead to genuine life-cycle environmental improvements at affordable costs.

Through consensus-based methodologies and decision-making, a fair and environmentally beneficial process for acquisition and procurement activities that satisfies the greatest number of stakeholders can be achieved. It is the purpose of the writers of this document to search out and nurture life-cycle–based approaches, both conceptual and quantitative, that afford transparent tools for reaching consensus.

4.2.7 Simplicity vs. complexity

Determining the environmental preferability of a product is a complex challenge, which in some cases may require a comprehensive life-cycle assessment, recognizing that full LCA capability is still evolving. In contrast to the complexity of objectively determining environmental preferability is the desire on the part of many acquisition and procurement personnel for a simple decision tool such as a list of approved products, a single attribute measurement, or a list of materials to be avoided, which would relieve them of the requirement for environmental expertise and difficult comparative evaluations. This dilemma cannot be totally resolved at this time, but by developing life-cycle concepts and objectively identifying key environmental characteristics, it is possible to begin the process of defining and evaluating environmental preferability for products.

4.2.8 Small business considerations

The cost and complexity of using life-cycle concepts and LCA methodologies for determining environmental preferability must not be allowed to unfairly disadvantage small business competitiveness in the acquisition and procurement process. This potential issue for small business is similar to the impact of various other aspects of the acquisition and procurement process, such as highly sophisticated performance requirements, extensive product qualification testing, and health and safety requirements. As a result, it is expected that the impacts of environmentally preferable procurement on small business can be addressed on the same basis as for these other procurement considerations.

4.3 Acquisition

The acquisition process described here is typical of projects within the federal government (for example, a weapons system project in the Department of Defense) ranging from multi-billion-dollar programs incorporating the latest technology to relatively minor equipment acquisitions. It is also representative of programs in other government departments and consistent with practices in the private sector. It might apply, perhaps with some tailoring, to product development projects as small as household appliances or toys. Life-cycle concepts find a natural home in the systems engineering aspect of acquisition program management and offer promise as tools supporting continuous improvement of the program's environmental quality. They can be applied in a progressive development from concept to specific detail over successive stages of the life cycle.

4.3.1 A closer look at an acquisition process the DoD process

The milestones and phases in DoD's acquisition approach are summarized below.

- Determination of mission need: Identify emerging threats and technical opportunities. Define functional performance not met through existing systems. Develop concept of operations including mutual support with other forces and systems.
- Concept exploration and development: Explore a variety of alternatives and define the most promising system concepts. Develop a proposed acquisition strategy and initial objectives for cost, schedule, and performance.
- Demonstration and validation: Demonstrate that the critical technologies can be incorporated into the system design with confidence. Prove that the critical processes are understood and attainable.
- Engineering and manufacturing development (EMD): Translate the most promising design approach into a stable, producible, and cost-effective design. Validate the production process. Conduct a test program to demonstrate satisfaction of mission need, operational performance requirements, and contract specifications.
- Production and deployment: Establish a stable, efficient production and support base. Achieve an operational capability that satisfies the mission need. Conduct follow-up testing to monitor performance and verify correction of deficiencies.
- Operation and support: Train and exercise forces. Support the system so it continues to meet mission need. Conduct operations. Identify shortcomings that require improved performance.
- Decommissioning and disposal[1]: Salvage reusable items and market recyclable materials. Remove hazardous components and dispose in compliance with legal and regulatory requirements. Close program-specific facilities.

The language of DoD guidance already embodies life-cycle concepts with regard to environmental parameters. However, specific tools for addressing environmental matters are not currently available to the DoD project manager. As a result, environmental issues are in principle an equal "partner" with other key areas to address under a Total Quality Management or Continuous Improvement philosophy, but in practice this equivalence has not fully occurred.

There has recently been increased emphasis on assuring that major defense acquisition programs' managers and their engineers have the responsibility to address the environmental implications of their system designs, to bring forward definitive descriptive data, and to reflect the significant costs from environmental effects in their life-cycle cost estimates.

---

[1] Not presently a formal part of the DoD acquisition process, though all the cited functions are performed routinely in the department.

Chapter 4: Acquisition and Procurement 57

The Army has highlighted the environmental area for project managers (Production Base Modernization Agency 1992). Revisions are in progress to reflect the latest use of life-cycle concepts:

"Sound environmental stewardship is a necessary component of all projects...Project Managers must be aware of the impacts their projects will have upon the environment and plan for them accordingly....Environmental expenses are now a cost of doing business and must be included in all phases of project planning. The costs of developing a sound environmental stewardship program and ensuring compliance are minimal compared to the costs of project delays, pollution cleanup and criminal penalties."

During the research and developmental stage, data are often predictive in nature and the life-cycle practitioners are often the chemists, process developers, engineers, and managers striving to identify the areas in need of further environmental emphasis. The resultant inventory is classified against the key categories in the impact assessment phase (usually not site-specific) utilizing characteristics such as safety, health, and ecological factors, along with a growing emphasis on resource depletion. Consequently, areas for improvement assessment can be identified and factored into the developmental program based on appropriate trade-offs of requirements, environmental burdens, and costs.

In the production phase, both the quantity and quality of the inventory analysis data is increased with commensurate broadening of the impact assessment phases to include more site-specific information associated with the need to develop detailed environmental impact assessments (EIA) associated with production facility design, construction, or operation. At this stage, a comprehensive LCA would be appropriate.

Among the myriad duties of a DoD program manager (PM) is development of a program life-cycle cost estimate (PLCCE) as part of the documentation for initial approval to proceed. At every subsequent major review, the PM presents an updated estimate reflecting all the improvements in program definition during the interim. In principle, this estimate should include all the significant costs to the government, from initial concept development through final disposal of materials remaining when the system has no further military use. In practice, the environmental costs regularly have escaped systematic attention in PLCCEs; instead, they have tended to emerge piecemeal as revealed through regulatory actions such as development of an environmental impact statement, application for a release permit, or response to a notice of violation.

The Cost Analysis Improvement Group (CAIG) in the Office of the Secretary of Defense is leading the DoD cost analysis community to take a more inclusive, forward-looking approach with the goal of capturing all significant environmental costs in the PLCCE as well as corroborating estimates prepared by the sponsoring military service and the CAIG itself. Since no one can estimate the cost of a program that is not adequately described, achievement of that goal critically depends on the PM reporting full assessments of the program's environmental content and impacts. The details of accomplishing that prescription in a sound, scientific, and comprehensive way may some day be served through a comprehensive LCA. But absent available technology for executing the complete LCA, the CAIG is seeking expedient measures for capturing at least the most significant environmental costs in the PLCCE and related estimates. Here, the use of life-cycle concepts can play an important role.

For many acquisition programs, the complexities lead to the need for a variety of tools to help the stakeholders in decision-making. Such tools could include models that incorporate the LCA methodology and databases that help quantify life-cycle costs. The use of modeling tools for all ingredients, components, manufacturing processes, use scenarios and disposal/demilitarization scenarios would benefit all life-cycle stakeholders (program managers, chemists, process developers, and production managers).

Identifying and addressing the total life-cycle cost is a significant, but not insurmountable, challenge faced by the PM with the same risks associated with technical decisions. Incorporation of life-cycle costing techniques or tools into the framework of the program manager's LCA activities is a viable and recommended approach.

> Chemical weapons as an example of unanticipated life-cycle effects
>
> DoD's history with chemical weapons offers a cautionary tale of how overlooking environmental effects during design and acquisition may impose important costs later. When those weapons were designed, the Soviet threat and strict secrecy combined to rivet attention on building the product and getting it to the field. At that time, the two accepted methods of disposal in routine use were ocean burial and burning in an open pit, neither of which, presumably, seemed very costly. President Nixon banned production of unitary chemical munitions in 1969, and the next year these traditional disposal methods were banned as well.
>
> Since then, the Army has managed a series of programs to destroy these munitions by various methods, principally high temperature incineration. The current program began with passage of legislation late in 1985 calling for destruction of the entire stockpile (with possibility for a small withhold) by September 30, 1994. Three extensions stretched that date to December 31, 2004. Total program costs have grown from an initial figure of $1.7 billion in 1985 to the 1992 estimate of $7.9 billion, the latter only for operations through December 2000. A new estimate will include the extension to 2004 as well as dismantlement of the destruction buildings themselves.
>
> Minimizing the risk of catastrophic accident certainly has much to do with the delays and costs. The designs of some munitions exacerbate the problems. In the most numerous munitions, the M-55 rocket, the chemical agent is in a sealed canister and cannot be withdrawn nondestructively; it has no valve. In addition, the munitions have an integral rocket motor that can be separated from the agent canister only by

> cutting. As a result, disposal facilities are constructed with 18-inch reinforced-concrete walls to withstand explosions; all operations are conducted under a negative pressure differential where the exhaust stream is treated with high efficiency scrubbers. Sophisticated, redundant safety features protect workers and the public.
>
> Since the environmental impact statement rules out transportation between sites as posing unacceptable risks, planning calls for using disposal facilities at Johnston Island, a small Pacific atoll, and eight domestic sites. Each location is burdened with its own tangle of local regulatory and public relations concerns; for example, each facility must obtain permits from the host state for solid wastes, air emissions and water emissions the General Accounting Office has raised the possibility that it may never be possible to satisfy the requirements of some states.
>
> Could this burden have been foreseen when these munitions were designed and built? The question might make for an entertaining debate, given the circumstances of the Cold War and a public not yet sensitized to the environment. However, what seems certain now is that today's public will not tolerate another weapon-system–related liability of this magnitude; such experience demonstrates that the DoD acquisition process needs a life-cycle orientation to wastes and their impacts.

4.3.2 System engineering approach the Saturn example

Saturn Corporation is also attempting to employ life-cycle concepts at multiple and early stages of the product development cycle applied both to manufacturing facilities and the product (cars) themselves. Using the systems engineering approach, life-cycle concepts assist in developing vehicle design guidelines that provide Saturn's product development teams information in the areas of processes, material selection, and design for disassembly.

Applications of life-cycle concepts at Saturn have produced the following results:
- Design materials selection is influenced by environmental concerns. Water-based paints, sealers, and adhesives that result in fewer emissions to the air are used, and polymers that can be reground and reused are used in the manufacture of the interior and exterior of the vehicle. Life-cycle approaches will be used to inform the decisions.
- An LCA of a typical Saturn vehicle is under development and will help guide decision-making.
- Numerous manufacturing process change were implemented based on life-cycle consideration.

4.4 Procurement of environmentally preferable products and services

4.4.1 Goal

Environmental improvement is the overall goal of procurement that encourages purchase of environmentally preferable products and services. In order to encourage the purchase of environmentally preferable products, we need to initially identify the desired environmental performance features of products or determine what constitutes an environmentally preferable product (see Section 4.4.2).

In order to have continuous environmental improvement, the process for determining environmentally preferable products must ensure that the needs of a rapidly evolving marketplace are also met. The current system of procurement relies on standards and specifications that may have the unintended result of freezing technology and innovation. One way to avoid this is to frequently revisit standards and specifications that are in place; however, this may prove to be costly as well as unrealistic, given the number of specifications. Thus, an approach that is adaptable and capitalizes on the market forces that drive innovation as well as environmental improvement is desirable.

The determination of environmentally preferable products must also take into consideration local conditions. For example, in the Southwest, scarcity of water may mean that a product or a process that is heavily dependent on water consumption may not be deemed environmentally preferable, whereas a product or service that has high solid-waste impacts may be more problematic for the landfill-scarce Northeast. This implies that flexibility must be built into the determination process that would empower local decision-makers to purchase products that meet their specific needs.

4.4.2 Environmentally preferred products and services

Life-cycle concepts can be used to establish criteria for identifying environmentally preferable products. Vendors report environmental criteria to governmental agencies in bids, and agencies, in turn, use them to help select a winning bid. Underlying the approach for identifying environmentally preferable products is a set of guiding principles:

1) Establish scientifically sound, yet simple, initial guidance.
2) Utilize a process that includes all affected stakeholder parties.
3) Utilize life-cycle concepts as fundamental starting points in the process.
4) Add environmental considerations to (but do not replace) the already established purchasing considerations, including cost, performance, and health and safety.
5) Focus criteria or guidance for environmentally preferable products on pollution prevention, reduced energy and material consumption, reduced air and water emissions, and reduced solid waste through source reduction and all forms of landfill diversion.

CHAPTER 4: ACQUISITION AND PROCUREMENT   61

6) Establish individual attributes that identify environmentally important characteristics of the specific product under consideration instead of attempting to collapse attributes into a single number.

Implementation of this approach could begin with pilot studies. As this is a new approach, the pilot process will no doubt be challenging and fraught with unforeseen obstacles, yet its benefits could be tremendous. It has the potential to place environmental considerations on par with cost, performance, and other factors currently considered in the purchasing process, in a viable manner. Furthermore, it relies on the marketplace and competition to create continuous environmental improvement. The key steps to developing pilot projects are these:

1) Select products to include in the pilot. The lead government agency and purchasing agency (these could be the same) set up a process for selecting the products that will be the focus of the study. Products selected should be described in terms of a functional unit. Products selected should meet these criteria:

   a) offer the greatest opportunities for risk reduction,

   b) be high in purchase volume and/or dollar amount for a particular agency, and/or

   c) represent a breadth of products and services from simple to complex.

2) Identify barriers and develop a strategy. What is essential for the pilot to work? Is there clear support from top management? What might prevent vendors from obtaining selected environmental information? What will encourage purchasing agents to use the environmental information in their decision-making, and how will they use it? These and many other questions need to be considered. Identifying barriers includes reviewing current bid specifications, procurement regulations, and policies that may pose problems. For instance, if the resulting bid process placed a significant burden on small businesses and limited their ability to participate in the bid process, this could undermine the success of the pilot. After identifying barriers, the agencies develop a strategy to manage them.

3) Identify stakeholders. For each product, the agency identifies the stakeholders that need to participate in the pilot study. This includes representatives from government, purchasing agencies, vendors, manufacturers, small businesses, environmental groups, taxpayer groups, and other interested parties.

4) Select key environmental considerations. Using life-cycle concepts, the stakeholders perform the following functions:

   a) Select the measurement criteria that represent the major attributes or characteristics of concern through a consensus process. Criteria include energy consumption, materials consumption (including post-consumer materials), air emissions, water emissions, and solid waste, as well as concerns such as biodiversity, toxics, and nonpoint source pollution.

SETAC Press

Stakeholders define the measurement criteria in numeric terms where feasible.

b) Identify the most critical stages in a product's life-cycle when the selected attributes make a significant impact on the environment. These stages will be the focus of data collection. This implies that data may not be collected from all life-cycle stages for a given product.

c) Determine data needs and availability. Where data are not available, the stakeholders would determine how to proceed. This could mean collecting new data; recognizing data gaps and proceeding, with the intention of collecting the data in the future; or discontinuing the pilot for the product in question.

5) Identify how pilot success will be measured. The lead agency identifies how the success of the pilot will be measured and determines how data collection needs will be met. If allowable, and pre- and post-surveys are going to be used, pre-surveys may need to be conducted at this time (for example, the agencies may want to examine the value of the educational and guidance materials for purchasing agents by conducting a survey to determine their current level of environmental awareness).

6) Modify bid specifications. The purchasing agency modifies bid specifications to include a section on reporting environmental measurement criteria, for the products included in the pilot. Agencies do not ask that vendors meet a certain standard but do expect vendors to be in compliance with any existing regulations. Vendors continue to submit information on prices and performance but now include information on the environmental considerations identified for the products in question. Information would be quantitative but might include qualitative information for unquantifiable considerations (e.g., biodiversity).

7) Develop educational materials, tools, and guidance. The lead and purchasing agencies develop education materials (training guide, video, program logo, reminders, fact sheets, etc.) tools (e.g., checklists, software, worksheets), and guidance (e.g., principles) that enable purchasing agents who review bids to make an informed decision. Ideally, purchasing agents who use the materials are actively involved in designing the materials and testing them. This is a very critical step because without education, training, and motivation, purchasing agents can ignore the environmental information that appears on bids or make an uninformed decision.

8) Conduct training. The lead and purchasing agencies conduct training sessions with purchasing agents. In situations where employees make purchasing decisions directly (they select the vendor rather than going to a common supply area), an educational campaign for employees is needed during the pilot.

9) Evaluate pilot and improve approach. The lead and purchasing agencies evaluate the pilot and find ways to improve the approach. Several iterations of

the process described above may be required to perfect the system into an approach that can be widely adapted and promoted. Over time, it is conceivable that environmental considerations will be standard information in bid packets.

The environmentally preferred product approach has several favorable features. First, information from the winning vendor's bid is available to competitors. This may motivate vendors and manufacturers to improve their products if they see that the winning bid reports better environmental measurements. Also, competitors could challenge the bid if the environmental measurements appear out of line. This approach encourages continuous environmental improvement, especially if the environmental considerations become key factors in determining the winning bid. Even if the environmental considerations are not the key factor for determining the winning bid initially (e.g., price or product performance can outweigh the environmental criteria in the purchasing agent's decision-making), vendors and manufacturers will be encouraged to improve their product because environmental considerations may be the determining factor in the future.

Second, decisions are made at the local level, allowing purchasing agents to account for regional resource and environmental variations that may fluctuate over time (e.g., a severe drought may make water use a higher priority for a limited period of time). A seal or declaration that a product is preferable is limiting because it reflects valuations at a particular place and time and cannot be quickly modified.

Choosing an environmentally preferable paper towel

This example describes an approach to establishing environmental criteria for the purchase of one commonly used product: paper hand-drying towels.

Background. The federal government purchases a significant volume of paper products, and paper towels used for hand drying represent a large percentage of this amount. The only environmental consideration in the government's purchase of paper towels is the requirement that all products meet a 20% minimum post-consumer recycled content standard. This example describes a process that would significantly expand the environmental considerations in the purchase of paper towels.

Establish functional unit. One of the most important considerations in any purchasing bid process is the establishment of the functional unit of comparison. The functional unit is a measure of performance that the unit delivers. For the paper towel example, this is a particularly important characteristic to establish because different paper towel products deliver different results (i.e., less absorbent products will require more towels to deliver the results of higher absorbency products). For this example, we will assume the functional unit of comparison is one hand-dry. Thus, in the bid process, suppliers would be expected to position the cost, performance, and environmental characteristics of their product on the basis of one hand-dry.

Establish products to compare. Ideally at this stage in the process, the procurement agent is given the freedom to consider alternate products or systems that deliver the same functional need. In the case of the paper towel system, alternative products or systems of interest may include hot-air dryer units or cloth towel systems. For the purpose of this example, we will assume that the purchasing agent has eliminated the consideration of hot-air dryers due to building infrastructure needs (i.e., these systems require electrical hard-wiring) and the cloth towel options have been eliminated due to the availability of built-in or already installed paper towel cabinets that would be too costly to replace. Therefore, this example is limited to considering only paper towels. It should be noted, however, that the analysis that follows would be acceptable for the evaluation of paper towels, cloth systems, and hot-air dryers; it would simply add additional attributes for consideration. Finally, the fact that existing infrastructure such as the availability of existing towel cabinets limits choices of the procurement agent at this point is a real problem; this demonstrates why considering these issues upstream of the final procurement process could afford greater potential opportunity for environmental improvement.

Establish stakeholder group. At this stage in the process, it is essential to establish and engage the affected stakeholder group. Doing so is necessary because this is the group that both needs to develop the fundamental information and to choose selection criteria (i.e., they have the data and knowledge); this is also the group that must utilize the resulting information in their decision processes. Stakeholders in the paper towel example include paper towel producers, users, procurement officers, and environmental groups.

Identify measurement criteria. After establishing some basic principles and group guidelines, the stakeholder group is charged with identifying measurement criteria for each environmental area of interest. To the degree possible, these criteria should be established measurements that are already in broad use in the industrial setting. Additionally, qualitative descriptions could be added to this list to cover areas of interest that are less developed scientifically. However, for this initial work, simplicity is an important element to consider.

During a stakeholder meeting of the paper towel group, the following broad areas of environmental interest represented as system inputs and outputs may be developed:

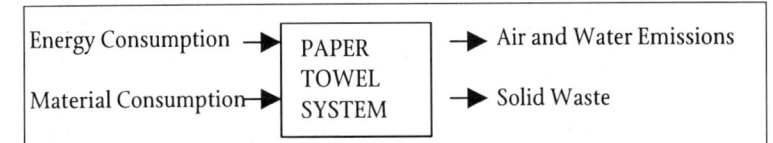

```
Energy Consumption  ──▶ ┌─────────┐ ──▶ Air and Water Emissions
                        │  PAPER  │
                        │  TOWEL  │
Material Consumption ──▶│ SYSTEM  │ ──▶ Solid Waste
                        └─────────┘
```

Against each of the inputs and outputs of the system, specific measurement criteria are developed. In the case of the paper towel system, the criteria established for initial considerations could include energy consumption, material consumption, air emissions, water emissions, solid waste, and RCRA hazardous waste.

Apply life-cycle concepts. At this point in the discussion, the stakeholder group specifically addresses the paper towel system, using life-cycle concepts. The focus of this effort is to apply the measurement criteria to paper towel systems in order to derive reporting areas of interest.

In the paper towel example, a number of life-cycle inventory studies have been conducted for a representative number of products in the category. This information and other evaluations effectively demonstrate that the manufacturing stage and the disposal stage of the paper towel system are the predominant points of environmental concern in the paper towel system. This assumes that the forestry practices of these suppliers are sound and further assumes that significant environmental differences do not exist between these practices. To be sure of this point, for those products that utilize virgin fiber as a material input to the system, a statement outlining forestry practices and potential environmental effects would be requested.

By utilizing life-cycle concepts, the stakeholder group now can focus on the manufacturing and disposal stage of the paper towel system to establish reporting areas of interest. First, in the energy consumption area, the major points of energy consumption in the system occur in the manufacturing stage and more specifically during pulping and paper-making. Additionally, the energy associated with the recycling process (collection, sorting, and deinking) needs to be identified. Further, since renewable sources of energy are less of an environmental area of concern, the stakeholder group can focus on the total amount of fossil fuel consumed in the system, regardless of fuel type.

Looking at the disposal stage provides additional insights. First, the amount of solid waste generated by the system both in terms of post-use waste (used towels) and deinked sludge (dry basis) are important considerations. Further, since the advancement of post-consumer recycling can be a policy objective, the amount of post-consumer recycled material (PCR) could be considered.

From a water emission standpoint, all the information from the pulp, paper-making, and deinking stage should be considered. Water emissions from other stages of the life cycle are not likely to be significant.

Finally, in regard to air emissions, the bulk of the emissions is directly related to the use of fossil fuel in the manufacturing process. Since fossil fuel consumption is already an area of interest, this information could serve to replace the need to track specific air emissions associated with fossil fuel use, and therefore, no additional system air emissions would be requested.

Report environmental information. At the end of the stakeholder review, each supplier interested in bidding on government paper towel business could be requested to provide the following environmental information in addition to cost and performance information:

> Energy consumption: Fossil fuel consumption (combined manufacturing & recycling processes only)
>
> Material consumption: None ; in addition to fossil fuel, fiber use will be derived if needed
>
> Air emissions: None; will not differ between alternatives, with the exception of fossil fuel-related emissions
>
> Water Emissions: Emissions from the manufacturing process (includes pulping, paper-making and deinking)
>
> Solid Waste: Total post-use solid waste (used towels), PCR amount into system, and deinked sludge on a dry basis

It should be noted that each of these parameters must be related to the functional unit, in this case, the towels needed per drying operation.

In addition to this information, the outline of forestry practices and potential environmental impacts could be requested. Obviously, this list could be expanded to include other qualitative criteria, as well as specific additional quantitative information.

Communicate, inform, motivate. Merely providing a vehicle for industrial reporting of these factors may not effectively initiate action. Therefore, it is helpful to develop and assess informational and educational tools such as computer aided spreadsheets, information, and education regarding local environmental areas of concern, as well as training and background materials. Further, motivational tools such as internal and external reward and recognition, as well as potential price

Chapter 4: Acquisition and Procurement

> preference for environmentally preferred products could be established.
>
> Strive for continuous improvement. Finally, a test market or limited roll-out of this concept could provide additive learning. In addition, an annual review of the paper towel category to review learning, adjust, add, or modify criteria or reporting needs seems appropriate.

4.4.3 Issues

The approach that is described in Section 4.4.2 leaves many unresolved issues. At the most basic level, the approach stops at the point of having identified characteristics of an environmentally preferable product. This does not necessarily mean that the product with those attributes will be purchased. Most procurement officials do not have the necessary training to make environmentally informed choices, nor should they necessarily be expected to bear this burden alone. Federal procurement officials serve the important role of "gate keepers" of materials that flow into the federal government; however, they are not necessarily the ones who decide what enters those gates. Requiring them to do so would add to their already overburdened set of tasks; it also runs counter to the decentralization of purchasing and the push for purchase of commercially available items. These initiatives, in effect, will mean that the division between purchaser and customer/user will become blurred, if not entirely eliminated, particularly for those products that can be purchased "off-the-shelf." Ultimately, the original requester of the product or service needs to do his/her part by specifying environmental preferability as a criterion. Initially, this may mean merely requesting that a product purchased has some desirable environmental characteristic.

Another issue is rooted in applying life-cycle concepts: information along the life-cycle stages, both upstream and downstream, may be difficult to collect and disseminate. Gaps in information may leave some significant causes of environmental harm out of the process. If none of the stakeholders has yet investigated a stage or process, it may be overlooked. Yet, consideration of the broad range of information, particularly of those stages in the life cycle that have been identified as being significant, is crucial in a preferability determination. One way to overcome this may be to establish a system for vendor "self-certification." There are two important aspects to this certification process. First, it could help create a chain reaction whereby information requested by the purchaser (government) of the vendor in turn can trigger a request by the vendor of their suppliers, all the way upstream to the raw material suppliers. It is recognized that, in reality, this desired effect may not occur and the flow of information may be far from perfect, e.g., if overseas suppliers are involved. Second is the importance of transparency. Supporting information should be made public.

Two related issues arise. First, who can "afford" to collect such information? Are small businesses likely to be put at a disadvantage over larger companies that may be better able to afford such information collection? The answer may be "no" in the manufacturing sector, because everyone is in a chain of supply; the further upstream one gets, the

SETAC Press

less likely that a small company is in the chain (e.g., raw materials acquisition is done mostly by large companies). On the other hand, it may still be very difficult for a small intermediate supplier with little economic "clout" to request this type of information from a large supplier. It may also be difficult for the service sector.

The second issue relates to how this information is effectively relayed to the decision-maker (whether it is to the stakeholder, procurement officer, or end user). One possible approach may be to adopt the format used in nutritional labeling, with the difference, however, that environmental information in this case need not be collapsed down into a "label," although a label certainly is one mechanism for communicating the information.

Another potential issue is the actual price for products and services. Currently many environmental costs (solid waste disposal, air pollution cleanup, etc.) are borne by society as a whole without a direct link to the goods and services that caused the problem or to the original purchaser. The environmentally preferable products approach could, in theory, shift the previously unaccounted-for environmental externalities up to the decision process. This could have the initial effect of increasing near-term costs for environmentally preferable products while reducing total life-cycle costs for cleanup.

Finally, the approach described in Section 4.4.2 takes for granted that a consensus can be reached by stakeholders and that vendors will participate when, in fact, neither may necessarily be true. This could be true for a variety of reasons, including unclearly stated goals or benefits that could accrue to the parties involved in the process. It will be important to ensure that agencies consider how to handle this type of situation.

4.5 Conceptual toolbox methods: applicable to acquisition and procurement

A variety of analytical methods, and related metrics and practices, are available for applying life-cycle concepts. A number of these have application at various stages of the acquisition process. Some are particularly well suited to enhancing procurement decisions.

4.5.1 Tools used in the acquisition process

Analytical tools (methods) represent part of a larger set of analytical processes that have potential utility at some point in the acquisition process. Life-cycle concepts, for example, can be applied at all stages of acquisition, from the earliest conceptualization of a system, to meet the identified needs of a particular stakeholder. Similarly, Design For the Environment (DFE) (Fiksel 1996) and Industrial Ecology (Graedel and Allenby 1995) approaches can be profitably applied to supplement traditional safety and environmental requirements reviews at concept exploration, demonstration, validation, and other stages and may help to refine more detailed decisions in later stages of the process. Material balance and chemical use mapping methods probably have their earliest application at the engineering and manufacturing development stage, while quantitative LCA and risk assessment are likely to become applicable in the later phases of this stage, as the data necessary to support these activities become available. It is important to note

CHAPTER 4: ACQUISITION AND PROCUREMENT 69

that all of these analytical methods can be brought to bear well in advance of actual procurement or production of goods and services, and ideally, they should be.

4.5.2 Tools applicable to procurement decisions

Ideally, in procurement, the need for analysis by the procuring agency is diminished because the organizations involved in the conceptualization and development of the goods and services to be procured have already engaged in such analysis. In practice, organizations that wish to protect the environment, avoid environmental liabilities, or profit through environmental efficiencies are likely to be faced with the need to undertake such analyses themselves for a considerable period.

All of the tools described above, with the exception of DFE, are potentially applicable in procurement. In practice, the most useful tools may be LCA (conceptual or quantitative), risk assessment, and material balance models, as these allow for the ready formulation of direct questions to immediate suppliers, including questions that can be forwarded to upstream suppliers.

DFE, chemical use mapping, and industrial ecology appear to have greater utility when applied to the larger universe of acquisitions, with its concomitantly greater range of potential interventions.

4.5.3 Economic accounting tools

Because cost is a natural consideration for stakeholders already involved in acquisition and procurement decisions, life-cycle tools that directly address the interaction between environmental considerations and cost considerations may have particular promise in convincing these stakeholders to address environmental issues. At least some of these stakeholders may have greater interest in avoiding undesirable environmental impacts, if it can be demonstrated that, by doing so, they can reduce the likely cost of an acquisition or procurement.

Life-cycle costing offers one approach for incorporating environmental considerations directly into cost calculations. By considering material and energy flows (from a life-cycle inventory) over an extended time period, costs and potential savings that may be neglected in conventional accounting can be addressed. These include factors such as trade-offs between initial device costs and energy cost savings, or the potential costs associated with closure and monitoring of hazardous waste disposal sites. This approach is applicable throughout the acquisition process but becomes increasingly more accurate at later stages.

Economic measures of environmental impacts associated with an acquisition or procurement tend to take one of two forms: direct expenses associated with environmental compliance or control measures, and indirect estimates of the economic implications of environmental damage. The former can include such items as the cost of pollution control equipment or the financial guarantees required to receive a permit for a landfill. The latter involves the use of economic modeling (and occasionally survey and interview research) to establish the value stakeholders put on such items as clean air and pristine

SETAC Press

wetlands. One approach might be to ask stakeholders to indicate their willingness to pay to avoid damage to such resources. Many others approaches exist and are discussed in a summary of impact assessment methods published by the USEPA (1995).

4.5.4 Non-economic metrics used in analysis

Each aspect of an industrial system has a set of associated metrics. Inputs can be measured in terms of energy use, consumption of stock resources such as petroleum (either directly or as an energy source), and consumption rates of flow resources, relative to their replenishment rates. Wastes and emissions can be characterized either directly as released masses or weighted by impact-related features such as chemical oxygen demand (COD), biological oxygen demand (BOD), or toxicity. Land use and ecosystem effects can be addressed by simple metrics, such as acreage lost to other uses, or by considering the characteristics of land use and the alternative land use that has been displaced.

In most cases, the metrics applied to these different features of industrial systems are not directly comparable. This disparity in metrics represents a long-standing problem in LCA, and one for which no satisfactory universal solution exists. Generally, except when environmental costs are calculated, it has been simply passed through the analytical process to be addressed in the valuation phase. Because acquisition and procurement processes require that decisions be reached, and consequently that valuation decisions be made, some solution to the metric problem must be accepted.

Table 4-1 presents a brief summary of some common metrics potentially associated with a system. Many more could be identified. The key considerations in employing such metrics in valuation decisions are that they are not directly commensurate and that for many impact categories only potential, not actual, impacts are measured.

There is grave doubt in the scientific community about the ability to meaningfully assign monetary values to the range of impacts considered by various life-cycle analytical tools, or to the far more limited range of effects considered in human health risk assessment. Most such monetizations, such as "cost per life saved," lose credibility through a failure to consider other significant aspects of toxicity, such as morbidity, and through naive assumptions regarding the scale properties of toxicity metrics (for example, there is no biological basis for the assumption that a twofold difference in the reference dose for two chemicals will be mirrored across a wider range of dose levels.)

The problem of comparing impacts becomes commensurably greater when different categories of impact, such as those described in Table 4-1, are compared. No successful objective scheme has yet been devised, even for limited problems such as comparing carcinogenic and non-cancer toxic effects. Thornier problems, such as trade-offs between releases of toxic chemicals and consumption of stock natural resources, have generally been left to the judgment of stakeholder groups on a case-by-case basis.

This approach to a common metric for disparate environmental effects may have applicability to large acquisition programs, at least in concept, but its utility for procurement decisions seems limited, given the time and funds necessary to complete such an exer-

CHAPTER 4: ACQUISITION AND PROCUREMENT   71

Table 4-1 Example non-cost metrics for life cycle

Normalizing variables	Stock input	Flow input	Emissions	Land use
Direct	Mass	Mass	Mass	Acreage
Mass	Proportion of known reserves	Consumption to production ratios		
Time	Time to exhaustion	Time to system breakdown	Rate of release	
Consequence			Inventory of concerns; toxicity scores	Displaced function; loss of critical function
Efficiency	Use per unit production or function			

cise. Even within the broad acquisition process, this approach may have limited practical utility.

In addition to the difficulties with metrics identified in life-cycle analytical techniques, it must be borne in mind that both acquisition and procurement processes have generally employed economic metrics (cost) as primary driving factors in decisions, once a system or set of systems has been established that meets designated performance criteria.

4.6 Implementation

New policies, executive orders, and even legislative mandates can easily go unheeded without effective communication, education and training, and implementation strategies that motivate and encourage participation. Program implementors (staff responsible for implementing changes) must address several essential elements to successfully implement life-cycle concepts into acquisition and procurement. This includes support from top management and purchasing agents, authority, resources, communication, incentives, education, training, tools to make the job easier and more feasible, and finally, measurement.

Top management support is needed to obtain initial authority to implement changes in acquisition and procurement procedures. Additionally, most stakeholders within the agency need to support new policies, in particular employees who face new responsibilities. To reach these audiences, program implementors can obtain information highlight-

SETAC Press

ing the policy's costs and benefits and can communicate this information in briefings and meetings.

Applying life-cycle concepts to acquisition and procurement is relatively new to government. In the federal government, authority to implement life-cycle concepts appears in Executive Order 12873 regarding environmentally preferred products and in other agencies such as DoD's Environmental Issues Over the Life Cycle: DoD 5000.2-M and System Engineering MIL-STD 499B discussed earlier in this chapter. In contrast, most state and local governments do not yet have broad, if any, authority, to implement life-cycle concepts. For these state and local governments, a first step is to seek an internal policy directive and in the longer term, if needed, to seek a legislative mandate that requires an agency or government to implement life-cycle concepts.

Resources in the form of funding, employees, and necessary equipment are basic to implementation. Soliciting adequate funding and staff time is an important goal for any implementor.

Communication is a challenge under the best of circumstances, even more so in a world where knowledge about environmental impacts of various products and services is needed to identify and purchase environmentally preferable products and services. Communications should strive to increase the flow of accurate, meaningful information about environmental performance of products. This needs to occur not only among vendors and purchasers but also among vendors and their suppliers. Given that the purchaser may not always be the end customer/user, it is important to have information flow between these two groups. The needs of each party also must be transmitted back up the chain so that there is a true push/pull dynamic.

New initiatives in government are often short-lived. A hot issue today is forgotten tomorrow. Implementors cannot simply inform, they must motivate, especially for voluntary programs. Some techniques to motivate employees include cash bonuses for measurable achievements that go beyond job requirements, awards, recognition, and privately revealed information on performance that compares an employee to a norm. Methods that might motivate vendors to provide information include price preference (savings from pollution prevention activities may be used to justify price preference), awards, and recognition.

An education campaign can ensure that employees are informed about new policies. It may be advantageous to describe changes in terms of expanding current acquisitions and procurement policies, so environmental considerations are on par with other criteria, rather than identifying changes as part of a new program. New programs pop up all the time and often fall down just as quickly. A team with representatives of target audiences can have the charge of creating a logo, slogan, contest, etc. that invite participation while educating.

In addition to basic educational materials, certain key players will need training. In the case of acquisition, this could involve all or key employees in the acquisition process, while procurement training may focus on purchasing agents and vendors. Training can be conducted periodically. A telephone hotline can be used to provide quick access to hands-on assistance. Training for new employees can be modified to introduce life-cycle concepts.

To supplement training, key players will need tools to make the job easier and more feasible. These tools might include worksheets, spreadsheets, or fact sheets, e.g., that provide quick reference or assist in performing calculations.

Finally, part of implementation is to measure and evaluate program success and make improvements. Evaluation can include both qualitative and quantitative information.

4.7 Summary of key findings

The following represents the key findings on the application of life-cycle concepts to acquisition and procurement processes.

1) Life-cycle concepts can play an important and nonredundant role in all phases of the acquisition and procurement process.
2) Life-cycle concepts can help to determine where the most appropriate intervention in the acquisition and procurement process should occur, what tools should be used, and what environmental impacts may result from acquisition and procurement decisions.
3) Life-cycle concepts can help to minimize future unanticipated life-cycle effects, as illustrated by the chemical weapons example.
4) Life-cycle concepts can be integrated into acquisition processes with potential gain.
5) Mutual interdependence exists among stakeholders, consensus, and valuation processes.
6) Pilot studies to demonstrate the use of life-cycle concepts in acquisition and procurement processes should be implemented.
7) Life-cycle concepts can be utilized in a process to select environmentally preferable products, as in the paper towel example.
8) Additional tools, metrics, and data will become available as pilot studies occur.
9) Implementation of life-cycle concepts is dependent on positive communication, education, and motivation.
10) A generic process for application of life-cycle concepts to public policy includes these steps:
    - Establish goals of public policy.
    - Involve stakeholders in applying life-cycle concepts.
    - Identify environmental attributes of interest.
    - Gather data; conduct assessment and pilot studies.
    - Communicate, educate, and motivate.

4.8 Future needs

Applying life-cycle concepts to the acquisition and procurement process will require additional development and, more importantly, immediate identification of pilot studies. The following sections outline some areas where additional development should occur.

4.8.1 Acquisition

Identification of specific tools and training, including life-cycle costing tools, is required to gain the broadest value from the deployment of life-cycle concepts. These tools should be pilot-tested and broadly disseminated to all interested parties.

4.8.2 Procurement

Identification of pilot products to evaluate and improve the suggested approach to environmentally preferable products is recommended as soon as possible. These pilot studies should be conducted on products that offer the greatest opportunity for potential environmental improvements and/or on products that are high in purchase volume and/or dollar amount for a particular agency. In addition, a breadth of products from simple to complex should be evaluated.

These pilot studies will identify the feasibility of the suggested approach, raise additional issues associated with metrics, and identify possible improvement opportunities. The output of these studies should be a recommended plan to implement the improved program widely.

4.8.3 Tools and metrics

At the present time, it would seem that only two alternative approaches to environmental metrics are feasible, although neither is fully adequate to meet the joint needs of environmental protection and rational acquisition and procurement. The first alternative is to completely separate environmental factors from cost factors, treating the environmental factors in a manner comparable to minimum performance standards. Such a process could independently set minimum acceptable levels for the various potential impacts of a system being procured (the establishment of such minimum criteria would occur earlier in the acquisition process). Any alternative that met these minimum standards would be deemed acceptable because no meaningful trade-off between environmental performance and cost could be calculated. Setting of minimum acceptable standards also avoids the difficulty of comparing disparate environmental impacts, as each type of impact could be addressed separately in setting minimum performance standards.

The other alternative is to adopt one of the more objective, yet admittedly inadequate, schemes for monetization, such as compliance cost (or avoided compliance cost). This alternative risks missing or miscategorizing significant environmental impacts for two reasons: 1) there is no meaningful common standard of environmental impact across different regulatory regimes, and 2) the cost of compliance may bear little relationship to the potential consequence of noncompliance. This approach does, however, permit the calculation of trade-offs between cost and environmental effects. Moreover, because this approach is compatible with standard decision processes used in acquisition and procurement, it may be easier to integrate into the acquisition and procurement process than a new set of separate environmental performance criteria would be. For the near term, compliance costing offers a high probability of avoiding significant disasters (environmental or financial) in an acquisition/procurement and provides a means for incorporating environmental considerations into the acquisition and procurement process, pending the development of more scientifically defensible metrics.

4.9 References

Consoli F, Allen D, Boustead I, Fava J, Franklin W, Jensen A, de Oude N, Parrish R, Perriman R, Postlethwaite D, Quay B, Séguin J, Vigon B, editors. 1993. Guidelines for life-cycle assessment: a "code of practice." Society of Environmental Toxicology and Chemistry (SETAC) and SETAC-Europe Workshop; 1993 Mar ; Sesimbra Portugal. Pensacola FL: SETAC Pr.

[DoD] Department of Defense. Environmental issues over the life cycle. DoD 5000.2-M

[DoD] Department of Defense. System Engineering MIL-STD 499B

Fiksel J. 1996. Design for the environment. New York: McGraw Hill.

Graedel TE, Allenby BR. 1995. Industrial ecology. Englewood Cliffs NJ: Prentice Hall.

Production Base Modernization Agency. 1992. Life cycle environmental guide for weapon systems project managers.

[USEPA] U.S. Environmental Protection Agency. 1995. Life cycle impact assessment. A conceptual framework, key issues and summary of existing methods prepared by Research Triangle Institute, EPA 452/R-95-002.

Chapter 5
Policy and Regulations

This chapter considers the role of life-cycle concepts in developing policy and regulations. The chapter addresses goal setting (Section 5.1), a general framework for applying life-cycle concepts in public policy (Section 5.2), a series of case studies (Sections 5.3–5.7), issues that may be barriers to using life-cycle concepts (Section 5.8), and international perspectives and recommendations (Sections 5.9 and 5.10). This chapter will not state conclusively that life-cycle concepts should be used in all public policy instances. However, it does suggest the limitations of policy and regulatory initiatives and documents some of the advantages of life-cycle concepts.

5.1 Goals of using life-cycle concepts in public policy

5.1.1 Goal

The goal of applying life-cycle concepts to public policy is to identify public policy opportunities for reducing environmental burdens associated with design, manufacture, use, and ultimate disposal of products, processes, or activities over the entire life cycle.

The assumption underlying the use of life-cycle concepts in public policy applications is that environmental improvement should address the entire range of potential impacts, from material acquisition to final product disposal. Considering only one life-cycle stage of a product may create unexpected impacts in another stage or another medium. To determine when and how one might achieve the most environmental improvement, impacts should be considered along the entire life cycle.

Life-cycle concepts can be applied at two levels:
- Conceptually, as a thought process that guides the selection of options for design and improvement
- Methodologically, building a qualitative/quantitative inventory of environmental burdens or releases, evaluating the impacts of those burdens or releases, and considering alternatives to improve environmental performance

In any application, LCA considers the environmental impacts along the continuum of a product's life from raw materials acquisition to production, use, and disposal (i.e., cradle-to-grave). The environmental impacts to consider include resource depletion, human health, and ecological health.

Life-cycle concepts expand the boundaries of an analysis to include cradle-to-grave or chain-of-commerce. They include a variety of environmental impacts, such as energy management, air releases, water releases, solid waste, material and resource management, and land use. They expand the potential environmental improvement options.

5.1.2 Observations

The case studies presented later in this chapter lead to a number of general observations concerning the use of life-cycle concepts in developing policy and regulations:

- Applications that combine voluntary and regulatory approaches will likely be more successful than those that employ only command-and-control approaches.
- Because many of the public policy applications using life-cycle concepts are driven by a combination of voluntary, regulatory, and financial forces, partnerships with the affected stakeholders will likely result in better implementation and improved environmental performance.
- Because much of the data and information pertain to company operations, it is important to solicit industry cooperation from the beginning of the development process and to respect issues related to confidential data.
- Public policies resulting from the application of life-cycle concepts require acceptance by all stakeholders, whose early and continuous participation is important.
- Application of life-cycle concepts could lead to more informed and comprehensive decisions because they consider a broad array of life-cycle stages and performance metrics.
- Definition of goals, determination of study scope, defining how information will be used, and specifying the user of the study must be done at the outset in applying life-cycle concepts. These decisions set the stage for the entire application and, if done properly, increase the potential for success.
- The application of life-cycle concepts to public policy is in its infancy. It is important to move at a speed consistent with proven and tested values and benefits. There is value in conducting pilot studies and then leveraging that experience in rulemaking applications. Once successful case studies have been developed, then their results can be leveraged to additional applications. The premise is to "Walk (and document successes) before you run."
- Although there are time and cost constraints in any initiative, it is still preferable to use life-cycle concepts in addition to traditional approaches to develop public policy.
- Although pollution prevention and multi-media approaches currently exist within government and industry, cradle-to-grave (life-cycle) approaches should be used to complement these existing approaches.

CHAPTER 5: POLICY AND REGULATIONS   79

This is particularly critical if all stakeholders (including upper management) are to understand and value the use of life-cycle concepts.
- One of the underlying values and powers of life-cycle concepts is that they present an operational mechanism that encourages a different overall conception of environmental protection, including a systems approach to a product's, process's, or activity's life cycle.

5.2 Generic framework for applying life-cycle concepts to public policy

Effective public policies address the entire range of potential environmental impacts along the chain of commerce (from material acquisition, manufacturing, and use to final disposal of used product) associated with the use of products, processes, or activities. Considering only one stage in the chain of commerce may create unexpected impacts in another stage or another medium. Therefore, impacts should be considered along the entire life cycle of product systems that are necessary to perform a specific function.

This section will present a generic approach to developing public policy, using broad systematic approaches. The generic approach has four components:

Component 1. Identify the purpose of the specific public policy application and what decisions are to be informed. During this scoping component, decisions that could likely result from the analysis are identified. The environmental benefits likely to result from the public policy and the tools or approaches best suited to address the intended public policy goal should be identified. Life-cycle concepts should be considered.

Component 2. Identify and solicit active participation and involvement of stakeholders. The affected government (federal, state, local), industrial, and public sector entities should actively participate in the development of the public policy.

Component 3. Identify and agree on key impacts and life-cycle stages to be included. The first objective is to identify the life-cycle stages and their potential implications for the public policy under consideration. The life-cycle concept becomes a framework to organize and focus the discussions and to provide a clear understanding of the issues under consideration.

The second objective is to reach an agreement on those environmental impacts that should be included. This is a crucial step. Consideration should be given to environmental categories, such as water, air, solid waste, energy, materials, and transportation, as well as to human health, ecosystems, and resource depletion. The ultimate direction of the public policy will include cost and social considerations as well.

Component 4. Present results, communicate, and motivate. The results of the analysis are discussed with the stakeholder group. The environmental improve-

SETAC Press

ment trade-offs are outlined. Ultimately, cost, technological, and social implications are considered in decision-making. Once the final public policy directions are agreed to by the stakeholder group, a communication strategy (originally developed during the third component) is reevaluated and implemented. Approaches to motivating the parties affected by the public policy are developed and implemented, including the following:

- Public policy awareness sessions for senior management in government, industry, nongovernmental organizations (NGOs) and universities
- Communication of case studies that demonstrate the value of the public policy, not only in the improvement to the environment but also in actual economic savings

This generic approach provides one way to develop public policy using life-cycle concepts. The next sections describe a series of case studies where life-cycle concepts have been used or are being used in developing policies and regulations.

5.3 Case study comparison of municipal solid waste management options using a life-cycle assessment

5.3.1 Background

The USEPA has initiated research that applies LCA methodology to evaluation of municipal solid waste (MSW) management options. The U.S. Department of Energy (DOE) is co-funding this research and will be a joint partner with USEPA in developing the technical information and conducting the LCA. The USEPA has received many requests for this research from both public and private entities, including the Conference of Mayors, the National League of Cities, trade associations, public interest groups, waste management industries, industry, academia, and research institutes. Other countries have initiated research programs to evaluate waste management options, including the United Kingdom, Canada, France, and Sweden, and have expressed interest in collaborating on a research program with the United States. In fact, results from an LCA of waste management strategies already are being considered by the European Commission in developing waste management directives.

The USEPA's Office of Research and Development will use an LCA to evaluate the environmental impacts associated with MSW generation, handling, transport, recycling/reuse, and disposal. This 3- to 5-year research project will include the collection of field data for developing emission factors and assessing cross-media transfers. Many municipalities and state governments have data collected during years of experience operating recycling and composting programs. In addition, new regulations under the Resource Conservation and Recovery Act and the Clean Air Act Amendments for MSW landfills and incinerators are either promulgated or are soon to be promulgated. These regulations have resulted in the collection of extensive data that will be used to develop the life-cycle inventory and conduct the assessment. However, the USEPA and DOE recognize that

CHAPTER 5: POLICY AND REGULATIONS   81

there are data gaps that can be filled only by collecting field data and conducting field test measurements.

The final output that is planned for this project is an expert tool for decision-makers that will allow them to use site-specific information regarding waste quantities and types, transportation requirements, energy characteristics, available markets, and waste management strategies to assess the relative impacts for the options under consideration. The project began in the summer of 1994 and, over the life of the project, will include a number of meetings with the stakeholders. In addition, extensive stakeholder review will be encouraged throughout the data collection process and the LCA. The following sections offer an evaluation of LCA's use for MSW applications.

5.3.2 Purpose

The purpose of conducting an LCA is to evaluate the potential upstream and downstream environmental impacts of MSW management options. The initial focus will be on management of plastics, glass, and paper. Additionally, the outcome of the LCA can help focus where costs may be incurred.

5.3.3 Definition of the problem

Currently, conflicting or incomplete information exists regarding the benefits and impacts of recycling, composting, landfilling, and incinerating. Management professionals are often forced to make decisions about waste management strategies without being able to look at the strategy as a whole and factor in site-specific information regarding available markets, transportation, and energy impacts. Concern has been raised that strategies are being adopted that may not be environmentally or economically preferable when site-specific and regional considerations are included in the evaluation. Additionally, the implications of various waste management options on the potential releases to the environment at all life-cycle stages have not been addressed.

5.3.4 Limitations of conventional approaches

The typical approaches used to evaluate waste options include risk assessments, cost-benefit analyses, and economic impact assessments. The primary limitations of these approaches include the following: 1) they frequently do not consider cradle-to-grave impacts (i.e., upstream and downstream impacts) for different media; 2) they frequently do not evaluate the options systematically; and 3) it is difficult to assess temporal and spatial variability. The following example uses light sources to illustrate the potential problems associated with a narrow perspective.

Programs are being established to encourage use of energy-efficient lighting systems, which use, in general, mercury-bearing light sources.
- USEPA's Green Lights Program, established in 1991, encourages companies to upgrade their lighting systems to more efficient sources.

SETAC Press

- Utilities are sponsoring demand side management (DSM) programs to reduce the demand for electricity.

However, because it is known to affect humans and the environment, mercury in the environment is a concern and reduction efforts are underway. It has been estimated that more than 17,000 tons of mercury are released annually into the environment from all sources. Depending upon where and how mercury release reduction is addressed, two possible and opposite directions might result. One possible option would be to ban fluorescent bulbs from landfills. This would result in increasing the use of incandescent bulbs, which contain little or no mercury; however, energy use would be increased while mercury in MSW would be decreased. Such a strategy would not reduce total life-cycle emissions of mercury. Life-cycle emissions of mercury would increase because the use and disposal of incandescent lights release, on average, about 4 to 10 times the mercury emitted by the use of fluorescent lights due to increased energy use from the combustion of coal. Incandescent bulbs require more energy to produce a given amount of illumination, and if the energy is generated by coal combustion, then mercury as a trace contaminant in coal will be released. In addition, when the entire life cycle is considered, other pollutants are reduced through the reduction of energy usage associated with fluorescent bulbs. USEPA estimates aggregated national electricity demand for lighting could be reduced by 50%, with annual reductions in emissions of CO_2 by 232 million tons, SO_2 by 1.7 million tons, and NO_2 by 0.9 million tons.

While this is only an illustrative example, it does indicate how alternative ways of collecting and analyzing environmental data and of defining system boundaries can improve the overall environmental quality of an operation, product, or process and can conserve energy, lower costs, and reduce the release of pollutants into the environment.

5.3.5 Value of life-cycle concepts to address this problem

The LCA methodology brings in elements that conventional approaches are not able to address. Even if a full LCA is not conducted, more informed decisions can be made using a life-cycle approach. For example, if waste option evaluations consider only the disposal and recycle options, then the conclusions may preclude source reduction or reuse. The LCA will allow consideration of raw materials acquisition, manufacturing, use, and all handling, transport, and disposal through a cradle-to-grave analysis (Figure 5-1). This approach represents the new paradigm for evaluating and developing processes, products, packages, and activities, which will provide for a uniform and systematic process to optimize three goals:

1) Reduce the consumption and increase the efficiency of use for nonrenewable energy and resources.
2) Increase the use of renewable resources and energy.
3) Minimize the releases of wastes from a specific system under study.

CHAPTER 5: POLICY AND REGULATIONS 83

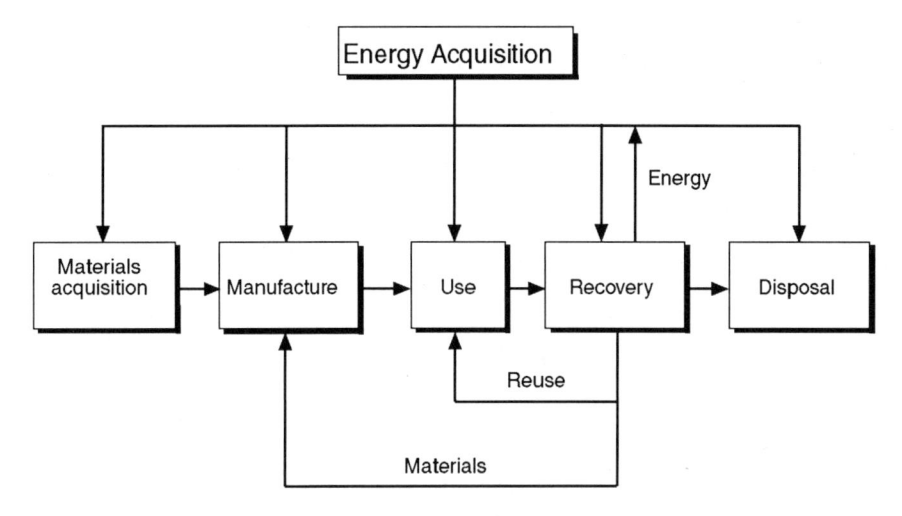

Figure 5-1   Life-cycle flows

The LCA's application to a paper waste stream provides, for example, an illustration of the value of a systematic approach to minimize environmental impacts. If the continued effort to push toward recycling as the single solution to our paper waste problem were increased to 80% recycling, then this continued push to recycle might in fact create greater emissions impacts (from energy consumption from transportation and the generation of power) associated with paper and the recycled products. There exists a level where it no longer is desirable to push the recycling goals higher. LCA will allow a systematic investigation of the trade-offs from several alternatives for solving the waste paper concern.

5.3.6 Obstacles

There are different views on the extent to which LCA can be performed at this time. However, success stories in Europe seem to suggest that it can be used for waste applications. LCA appears to be the best available tool for evaluating the potential upstream and downstream impacts for different process units (Figure 5-2). The linkage of these process units in the type of flow diagrams that are depicted in Figure 5-1 will be used to analyze the upstream and downstream impacts of different waste management streams.

One of the challenges will be to think beyond the waste generation stage of the life cycle and include the entire life cycle of products that ultimately enter the waste management stream. Concentrating solely on the waste stream limits the value of applying LCA. The fundamental consideration is that components in the solid waste stream are made up of individual products or packaging. This recognition and its implication for this application are critical. Additional obstacles with using the LCA for this application will be to reach a consensus with the stakeholders on the scope, boundary conditions, and research outputs, and to

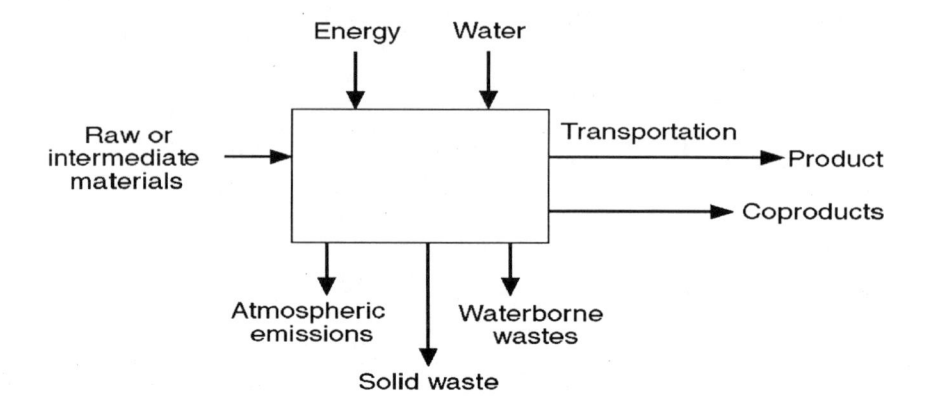

Figure 5-2   Material and energy flows in a unit operation

develop emission factors for the different unit processes. Budget and resource constraints will probably limit the extent that a full LCA can be conducted and the number of waste streams that can be evaluated. In addition, it will be difficult to account for the temporal and spatial variability that exists and to develop the media-specific data for each individual process unit.

5.3.7 Overcoming obstacles

It is important to involve stakeholders early in the process of conducting a LCA. By working to develop partnerships with the stakeholders, it is hoped that data and other information can be collected more effectively. For example, the paper, plastics, and glass industries may be willing to provide LCAs on their products, which would provide the information needed to perform a cradle-to-grave assessment. It is also thought that partnerships with the stakeholders in achieving the objectives of this research will result in its success.

Additionally, it is recommended that the research be phased by limiting the number of products that are evaluated. For example, paper may be a good candidate to start with because it can be applied to most, if not all, of the waste management strategies.

5.3.8 Communication

It is important to establish an early dialogue with the stakeholders, reaching agreements on the LCA scope, boundary, and limitations. A number of interim deliverables will provide extensive internal and external review of the LCA inventory, data, analysis of data, and implementation of the LCA. It is important to provide information for upper USEPA management about the progress of this research. If the project is successful, it will demonstrate that LCA is beneficial in developing policy options that will ensure protection of human health and the environment and conservation of resources.

SETAC Press

5.4 Case study: USEPA waste minimization and combustion strategy

5.4.1 Introduction

In 1993, the USEPA announced a draft Waste Minimization and Combustion Strategy to address the risk posed to human health and the environment by the combustion of hazardous waste. The USEPA hopes to encourage safe hazardous waste disposal practices and ultimately to reduce the production of hazardous waste. USEPA has plans to address these issues with regulations and voluntary programs. USEPA currently is considering revised emission standards for hazardous pollutants and metals such as dioxin, particulate matter, mercury, hydrochloric acid, and products of incomplete combustion (PICs). Also, USEPA is considering a number of voluntary initiatives to encourage waste minimization programs.

5.4.2 Purpose

This section describes how the USEPA may or may not benefit from using life-cycle concepts to better understand the issue of waste minimization and combustion in the United States and subsequently to address the risks posed by it.

5.4.3 Limitations of conventional approach

USEPA in the past has used RIA (cost-benefit analysis), cost effectiveness, market studies, waste flow analysis, risk assessment, consensus building, and other tools to understand how its regulations and voluntary programs will impact human health and the environment. Tools being used to understand environmental impacts of the combustion of hazardous waste are economic impact analysis, RIA, and risk assessment. These tools consider the cost, benefits, and risks posed by each disposal option and provide the policy-maker with information to make an informed policy decision. In the case of hazardous waste disposal, options include waste minimization, recycling, combustion, and hazardous waste landfilling. The tools currently being used will include financial and social costs, benefits such as avoided cancer cases and other avoided health effects, and the estimation of human and ecological risks posed by various hazardous pollutants as a result of combustion.

While each of these tools is beneficial to understanding the combustion industry and other waste management industries and the risks posed by them, none of these tools considers the cradle-to-grave" or life cycle of hazardous waste generation to hazardous waste disposal. Neither do these tools consider multi-media trade-offs or provide the policy-maker with a systematic approach to addressing adverse impacts to the environment. USEPA may benefit from using an additional tool such as LCA to capture the full life cycle of hazardous waste management.

5.4.4 Value of life-cycle concepts
The advantages of life-cycle concepts in examining combustion are these:
1) Life-cycle concepts can provide a more comprehensive picture of the interaction of combustion and waste minimization with the environment.
2) Life-cycle concepts contribute to the understanding of the overall and interdependent nature of the environmental consequences of combustion and waste minimization.
3) Life-cycle concepts provide policy-makers with information on the environmental effects of combustion and identify opportunities for environmental improvements such as waste minimization.

As is in the MSW management case study, LCA cannot be fully applied to the hazardous waste management case study. However, life-cycle concepts are ready for use in the case study. Approaches such as life-cycle inventories and stakeholder meetings could probably reveal opportunities for the reduction of hazardous waste production to USEPA.

Therefore, USEPA could describe the system of hazardous waste disposal as a system where each process — including the generation process, the transport process, the fuel blending process, and the disposal process — is defined as a set of operations performing a function. The flow of waste from "gate to grave" would be defined not only in terms of its function but also in relation to its inputs and outputs, thereby describing the upstream and downstream operation of hazardous waste disposal (Figure 5-3). The use of these concepts can therefore provide USEPA with data that describe the upstream and downstream effects of hazardous waste management.

In the case of hazardous waste combustion, applying the gate-to-grave or life-cycle concepts to hazardous waste management will 1) describe inputs such as process energy, fuel energy to generate electricity, and transportation energy; 2) describe air, water, and hazardous waste emission levels; and 3) describe outputs such as hazardous waste and products such as portland cement.

5.4.5 Obstacles
Although there are clear applications of life-cycle concepts to hazardous waste disposal, implementation will still be an obstacle. There will be some difficulty in defining the hazardous waste disposal system. Where do we draw the boundaries? Do we draw them at the point of hazardous waste generation, or do we begin during the manufacturing process or at raw material extraction? USEPA would need to answer these questions in order to clearly define the system and its boundary. Also, USEPA may find it difficult to integrate the RIA with the impact assessment. Finding consensus among the affected stakeholders such as the commercial and on-site incinerators, cement kiln companies, boilers and industrial furnace companies, fuel blenders, treatment and storage facilities, landfill opera-

CHAPTER 5: POLICY AND REGULATIONS

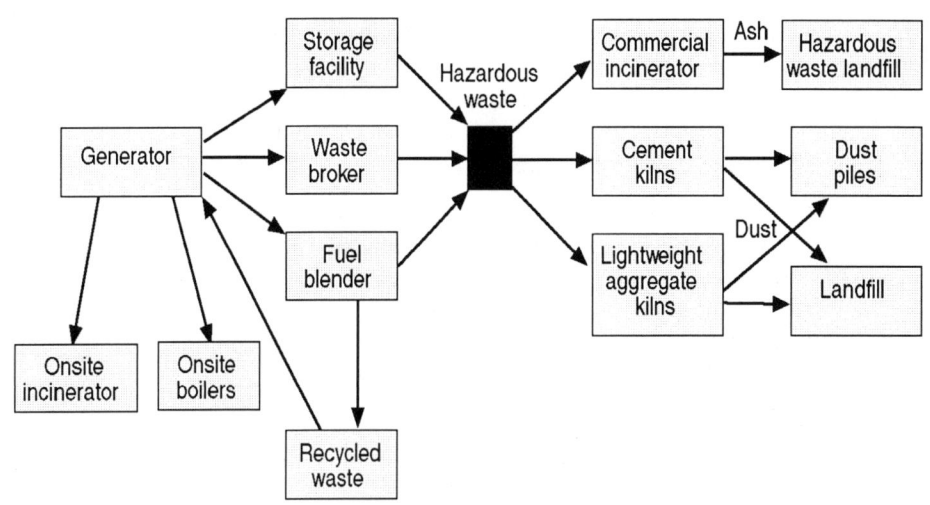

Figure 5-3   Life-cycle inventory template

tions, public interest groups, and the public, all of whom have diverse opinions, would be a challenge to meet. Given the uncertainty regarding and the lack of applications of life-cycle concepts to public policy, budget constraints and time commitments may also present obstacles to their implementation. Life-cycle concepts can be applied to this case study at a more qualitative level, but the question remains whether USEPA can apply them in practice in voluntary and rulemaking efforts.

5.4.6 Overcoming obstacles

Building partnerships among all the affected stakeholders is a key to overcoming many of the obstacles mentioned above. By involving stakeholders early in the public policy process and by opening lines of communication through regional and national public meetings, workshops and conferences, and opened and closed meetings with government, consensus may be achievable. Once consensus has been reached, the process of developing the system, the scope, the boundaries, and the inputs and outputs under consideration is possible. Also, consensus-building among stakeholders could resolve budget constraints because presumably industry, public interest groups, and government together could provide time and resources for achieving the goal of waste minimization.

5.5 Case study USEPA industrial laundries effluent guideline

5.5.1 Background

The USEPA's Office of Water is responsible for developing effluent guidelines and standards, under authority of the Clean Water Act, that use available technologies to limit the releases of specific pollutants in various industrial categories.

One of the effluent guidelines currently under development by USEPA is for industrial laundries (IL). Industrial laundries supply laundered work uniforms, wiping towels, gloves, flame-resistant clothing, dust covers and cloths, and similar items to industrial and commercial users (USEPA 1989). During the rulemaking process, USEPA continually refines the scope of the IL industry.

As part of the IL rule, the Office of Water characterizes effluents from facilities that launder wiping towels (including printer towels, shop towels, and industrial wipers) for reuse. These towels contain solvents, oil, and grease that are used in cleaning and finishing operations. The oils, solvents, and greases contribute to the pollutant loadings in discharges from industrial laundries to publicly owned treatment works (POTWs).

USEPA is concerned that pending IL regulations may cause a shift from the use of wiping towels to disposable towels, which would result in a transfer of pollutant loadings from water to landfills.

5.5.2 Purpose
In developing the IL effluent regulations, USEPA's Office of Water has decided to use life-cycle concepts and principles to identify relative environmental tradeoffs between disposable and laundered wiping towel options, including potential upstream and downstream environmental impacts.

5.5.3 Limitations of conventional approach
None of the regulatory approaches currently in place in the effluent guidelines process encompass a complete cradle-to-grave approach. Although USEPA uses many tools (such as RIAs and environmental assessments) to consider the environmental and economic advantages and disadvantages of all proposed options, none of the tools is capable of going as far downstream or upstream as an LCA does.

5.5.4 Value of life-cycle concepts
Because of USEPA's interest in approaching the IL wiping towel issue using a cradle-to-grave framework, LCA was viewed as an excellent tool to combine with ongoing regulatory efforts.

Various alternatives for treatment of wiping towels will be examined. Possible scenarios include (but are not limited to) these:
- Incorporating low-level treatment of wiping towels before laundering
- Incorporating best available controls to reduce pollutant levels in the final effluent
- Switching to disposable wiping towels
- Incorporating pollution prevention options in the use stage

CHAPTER 5: POLICY AND REGULATIONS

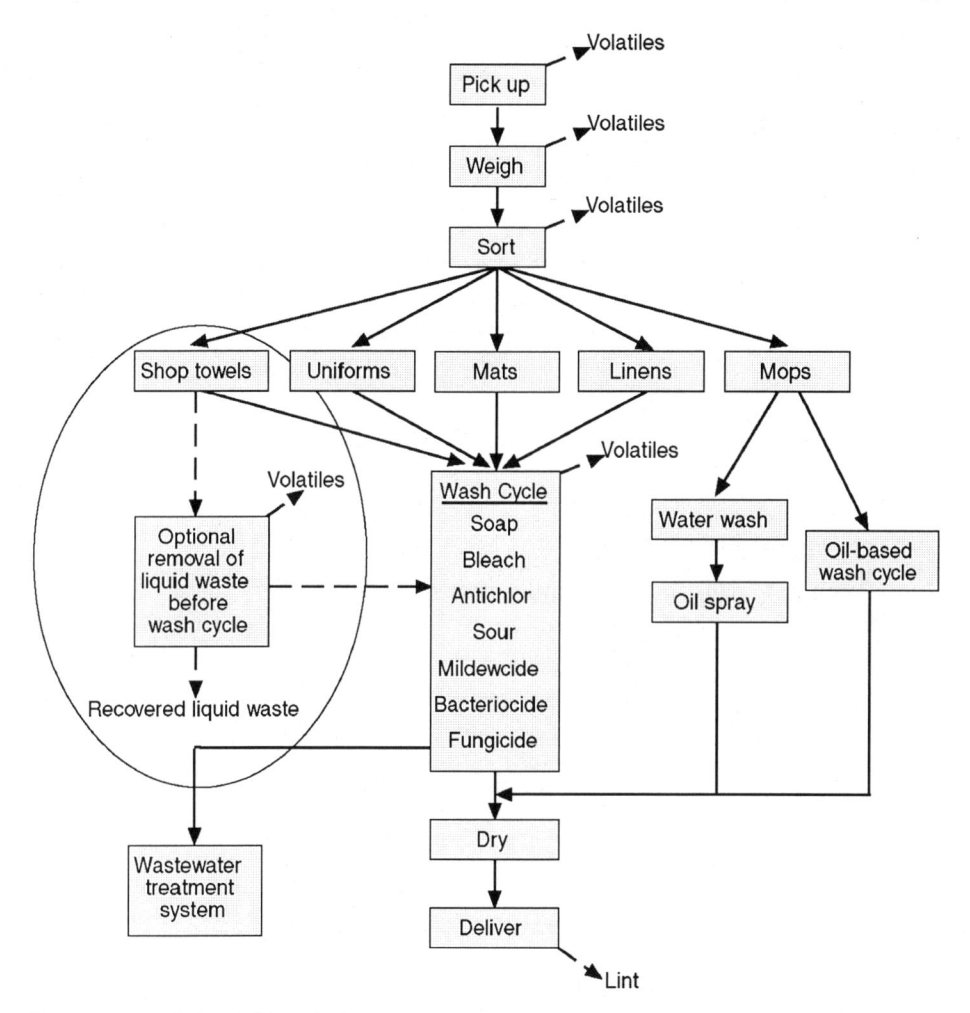

Figure 5-4   Industrial laundering process

The scope and boundaries of the LCA for reusable and disposable wiping towels have not yet been determined, but an initial process flowchart for IL has been developed (Figure 5-4). A stakeholder panel, potentially including representatives from various offices within USEPA, the IL industry, textile and paper industries, wiping towel customers, environmental organizations, and trade associations will be formed to discuss the LCA's purposes, boundaries, and goals. USEPA envisions conducting an LCA based upon the life-cycle stages, data categories, and impact categories relevant to the purpose and agreed to by the stakeholder group.

The life-cycle inventory methodology is sufficiently developed for this task. However, the impact assessment methodology is not as well-defined. Even with these limitations, incorporating life-cycle concepts can help ensure conformance with

SETAC Press

USEPA's goals of encouraging pollution prevention and a multi-media approach while also identifying areas for environmental improvement and resource conservation.

5.5.5 Obstacles and overcoming obstacles

As with any LCA, defining the scope and boundaries can be difficult, and with multiple stakeholders, may become a contentious process. Stakeholder participation and agreement can be facilitated by having a goal of environmental improvement of both reusable and disposable wiping towel options as opposed to establishing a preference of one option over another.

Stakeholders may be wary of LCAs both due to uncertainty surrounding the methodologies and the perception that LCAs are data-intensive and burdensome to regulatory efforts. Educational efforts (for example, showing that by broadening consideration of environmental impacts, LCA could aid development of rules that are likely to avoid media shifts), accompanied by frequent progress updates, can assist in supporting the LCA process.

The collection and use of confidential data may be necessary during the course of LCA. Utilizing USEPA confidential business information procedures that are already in place can ensure confidentiality while enabling the LCA to progress.

5.5.6 Communication

Presentation and communication of the study methodology and results are important in any LCA. Since initiating the industrial laundries rulemaking process in 1992, USEPA has involved several stakeholders, including trade associations, the IL industry, environmental groups, and other offices within USEPA. The incorporation of LCA into the rulemaking process will necessitate the inclusion of IL wiping towel customers, the textile industry, and the paper industry, as well as the stakeholders already participating. Involving all stakeholders in the LCA planning phases should ensure agreement on any limitations of the LCA, avoiding disagreement and unmet expectations after LCA initiation. Because goal definition and scoping occur throughout the LCA, frequent communication with stakeholders is necessary to take stock of progress to date, and discuss future courses of action.

In the IL rule, it will be important to acknowledge limitations of the study boundaries (once they are determined), indicating what is and is not included in the study, and limitations of the LCA results. Again, having input from all stakeholders is critical. Finally, presentation of results for wiping towel options should include data that are transparent and consistent with the study's methodology. SETAC's Guidelines for Life-Cycle Assessment: A "Code of Practice" (SETAC 1993) provides further guidance on presentation and communication of LCA results.

5.6 Case study: incorporating LCA concepts in a degreasing rule

5.6.1 Background

The Clean Air Act Amendments (CAAA) of 1990 directs the USEPA Administrator to promulgate regulations for 189 hazardous air pollutants in support of National Emission Standards for Hazardous Air Pollutants (NESHAPs). Section 301 of Title III states that promulgated emission standards for new or existing emissions sources of hazardous air pollutants shall "require the maximum degree of reduction in emissions of the hazardous air pollutants subject to this section (including a prohibition on such emissions, where achievable) that the Administrator, taking into consideration the cost of achieving such emission reduction, and any nonair quality health and environmental impacts and energy requirements ...."

Thus, this section of the CAAA directs USEPA to consider nonair impacts as well as air impacts of its regulations. It also directs USEPA to consider methods of preventing pollution as well as routine pollution control methods for achieving emissions reduction. Regulations promulgated are performance-based, determined by available technologies, rather than exclusively risk-based.

5.6.2 Purpose

In 1993, USEPA's Office of Pollution Prevention and Toxics (OPPT) initiated a study to explore methodologies for incorporating life-cycle concepts into rulemaking activities under the CAAA, using the degreasing NESHAP (a rule which was forthcoming at the time of project initiation) as a case study (Shapiro et al. 1993). As envisioned, life-cycle concepts could be used for assessing various regulatory options related to degreasing using chlorinated solvents, aqueous and semi-aqueous systems. By broadening the scope of environmental impacts considered, life-cycle concepts could provide the opportunity to align rulemaking with federal, state and industry emphasis on encouraging pollution prevention and avoiding cross-media shifting. Life-cycle concepts could also aid in identifying rules that are likely to avoid future revisions necessitated by a failure to achieve the maximum risk reduction guidelines contained in the CAAA.

5.6.3 Limitations of conventional approach

Several tools are used for evaluating the environmental impacts of regulations including environmental impact statements (EIS), risk assessments, and RIAs, which assess the benefits and costs of environmental regulations. Environmental data routinely collected in these analyses are more limited than life-cycle inventories because cradle-to-grave emissions are not determined. An RIA was not being prepared for the degreasing rule since it is classified as a non-major rule. RIAs are required only for regulations that are considered "major" based upon the following criteria: 1) the regulation is likely to have an annual effect on the economy of $100 million or more; 2) the regulation is likely to cause a major increase in costs or prices for consumers, individual industries, federal, state, or local governments, or geographic regions; or 3) the regulation is likely to result in significant adverse effects on competition, employment, investment, productivity, innovation, or on the ability of the United States-based enterprises to compete with foreign-based enterprises in domestic or export markets. EISs and risk assessments are not performed for NESHAPs.

5.6.4 Value of life-cycle concepts

Life-cycle concepts provide a broader assessment of environmental impacts by including upstream raw material requirements (which may not be quantified by some other tools) and potentially capturing upstream impacts by including upstream life-cycle stages.

OPPT wanted to ensure that in addition to various control options for degreasers, the NESHAP rule would evaluate alternative cleaning systems (both aqueous and semi-aqueous). As USEPA was interested in assessing environmental trade-offs between chlorinated solvent degreasing (which gives rise to air emissions) and alternative cleaning systems (which generate water emissions), life-cycle concepts and LCA were viewed as tools for expanding the regulatory analysis.

5.6.5 Applying life-cycle concepts

The types of data required by NESHAPs proposed under the CAAA and data required by LCAs were compared to determine if, and what type of, new information may be needed for applying LCA to rulemaking. Because rulemaking activities are encompassed by a legislative framework, the goal was to work within this framework, while expanding the analysis to make it more comprehensive.

While a full LCA for degreasing and alternative cleaning systems would include all the life-cycle stages required for producing, using, and disposing of cleaners, it is important to apply LCA within the time constraints identified in the rulemaking process. Because the availability of data necessary for an all-encompassing LCA may be limited, the decision was made to limit the application of LCA concepts to the downstream stages including environmental releases from cleaning systems and energy use and emissions from energy systems.

5.6.6 Obstacles

Three main obstacles were faced by this study. First, concerns were raised that the use of LCA would further burden the already rigorous process of rulemaking. The schedule for conducting a streamlined LCA was delayed while these concerns

CHAPTER 5: POLICY AND REGULATIONS   93

were addressed through discussions to explain LCA and its potential benefits to the rulemaking process.

Second, the time frame for completing the degreasing rule was short. Given the delays, it became obvious that the study would not be completed in time to make an impact on the degreasing rule.

Finally, USEPA funding for the entire project was not secured before project start-up. As a result, work was completed in a piecemeal fashion, further delaying its completion.

5.6.7 Lessons learned
This case study shows the importance of educating the many stakeholders involved in LCAs prior to project initiation. Additionally, to the extent possible, financial commitments should be secured before the study is started.

5.7 Case study: Dutch system for continuous environmental improvements in consumer products

5.7.1 Background
This case study examines the use of life-cycle concepts and LCA in the partnership between the Netherlands government, the citizens, and the consumer products industry. The system is based on an integration of regulatory controls and voluntary market incentives. The case studies described in the previous sections applied LCA to existing policy and regulatory questions. The Dutch government has established a whole new set of goals and partnerships.

This new policy is necessary because extensive government actions taken so far do not lead to sustainable development. The single-media or single-issue regulatory approach is not very effective with diffuse sources of environmental burdens. In addition, existing approaches often create new environmental problems by moving a pollutant from one environmental medium into another. This was one of the reasons the Dutch government developed a product policy, based on life-cycle concepts, that looks at all media. Existing policies may increasingly be influenced by the implementation of this product policy (Dutch Ministry of Housing, Spatial Planning, and the Environment 1994). However, this case study concentrates only on the product policy as it existed at the time of this workshop.

5.7.2 Purpose
The Dutch policy (Dutch Ministry of Housing 1994) begins with a clear goal statement that names the partners and basic principles.

"To bring about a situation whereby all the market actors — producers, traders and consumers — are involved in an ongoing effort to reduce the impact which products have upon the environment."

SETAC Press

The Dutch policy is based on the principle that all products have some burden on the environment. Regardless of how small or how great the burden, there is room for improvement. This is also the basic principle of continuous quality improvements familiar to successful companies. The most successful programs for improving environmental or quality performance are continuous systems that involve input from as many stakeholders as is practical. Because of the diversity of products and processes, defining ways to improve is most efficiently done by those who understand their own system. The challenge is defining a strategy that can both activate the expertise within each company and put the focus on the major improvement opportunities. The LCA concept of cradle-to-grave scientific analysis gives industry and the public some confidence that the most important environmental burdens can be identified.

Responsibilities for understanding the environmental burdens as well as actions that lead to continuous improvement are assigned to the entity that brings the product to the market. Equally important are shared responsibilities with consumers. The consumers' part includes choosing products that meet their personal and environmental standards. In addition, the consumer can help by using and disposing of the product appropriately. The government shares the responsibility for the reliability and the comprehensibility of information on a strategic level by defining regulatory processes. This system depends heavily on educated decisions by suppliers, producers, government, and consumers. However, the strategy does not depend on everyone becoming an expert. The producer must be the most knowledgeable. The government needs to have the expertise to track improvements and claims based on LCA and to educate the public. The consumer needs to be aware only of the basic issues.

5.7.3 Limitations of conventional approach

Existing problems have been the focus of past environmental regulations, and the minimum-standard–setting approach does not encourage improvements. Uncertainties in future regulatory direction may make it foolish to spend money on new improvements. These were seen as a major problems with conventional approaches. In addition, the single-issue focus may solve one problem but create or aggravate a different problem. Environmental trade-offs between different media or stages of the product life cycle cannot be critically compared with a single-issue approach.

5.7.4 Value of life-cycle concepts

The major advantage of LCA is that it helps to point out areas that may produce the biggest improvements. Given the overall policy goal, this makes LCA an obvious first choice as an analysis tool. Other instruments have limitations, as does LCA; however, LCA has a broader scope and may do a better job of setting the direction for improvements. Another major advantage is the long-term vision the LCA policy gives environmental regulations. Industry has more confidence in

CHAPTER 5: POLICY AND REGULATIONS   95

the long-term direction of regulations and can therefore make improvements based on logic and predictability.

5.7.5 Obstacles
The following obstacles were identified:
- Methodology issues. The inventory methodology is well developed. However, the impact methodology has not achieved the same level of consensus necessary to make public policy decisions. This is not necessarily a limiting factor. For example, there are still many opportunities to reduce environmental burdens that do not require sophisticated impact methodology.
- Uncertainties in the assessments. The degree of uncertainty in LCA may cause problems for some organizations when they have to make decisions. But small risk generally results in small gains. The Dutch system drives these decisions into the free marketplace, where large risks may lead to significant rewards.
- Data availability. Data availability is not consistent for all applications. Not all producers of materials or products put the same effort into collecting LCA data. In addition, some countries have not emphasized the environment; they are in the early stages of LCA and environmental awareness. Competition is helping to drive the latecomers into the LCA system. If one supplier will not supply LCA information, another one may. In the Dutch system, the company that supplies LCA data has a competitive advantage. In addition to data availability issues, there are differences in the complexity of data required for products. The single-material product (e.g., a grocery bag) will have a much simpler LCA than a complex product (e.g., a computer). These differences make it necessary to allow for time lags between various products.
- Resource limitations (time, money, and expertise). Large companies may be able to produce LCA data for their simplest products in a relatively short time. The money and other resources required for each study will naturally result in time lags for completion. This a logical outcome of the LCA process and is supported by market forces. Of course, a public issue may accelerate interest in the LCA of a specific product, regardless of costs. For some small and medium companies, data collection is more of a problem. However, much of the information these smaller companies require can be obtained from suppliers that are large companies. The smaller companies still must use their limited resources to study their own process, but, again, competitive forces will not allow them to put off this "investment" for long.
- Market forces. The major assumption in the Dutch model is that the market forces will drive environmental improvement. In other words,

SETAC Press

will environmental performance be valued by the consumer? We know that some consumers will be interested, but will enough use their buying power to make a difference? The education of the public plays an enormous role in changing consumer values. In addition, there is a secondary way improvements may be driven by the market. For many companies engaged in environmental improvements, the reduction of waste and energy has led to economic advantages in the marketplace. [Editors' note: Modifications of the Dutch product policy in late 1995 led to an emphasis on this latter approach.]

- Voluntary vs. regulatory issues. "If it is felt that the net effect of self-regulation has been unsatisfactory, and it has become apparent that this is the result of a lack of commitment on the part of the business community, then from 1-1-1998 as a last resort the legislation in place will also be used to introduce an obligation to provide product information." (Dutch Ministry of Housing, Spatial Planning and the Environment 1994) This aspect of the Dutch policy begs some questions. How will progress be measured? What will define "unsatisfactory"? If public education is not successful, how does that reflect on LCA?

- New product design. It will be some time before engineers understand how to weigh the different aspects of LCA data for product design. To accelerate this necessary knowledge growth, technical universities have been given funds to develop education programs for engineers, generating much interest among students.

5.7.6 Overcoming obstacles

The methods for implementing this policy in the Netherlands includes the following elements.

- Partnerships. The most promising method for overcoming obstacles is the forging of partnerships. Industry, government, and consumers all have responsibilities that are clearly defined. None can carry out their part without the support of the others.

- Market forces. The free market is the primary force used to drive improvements. This solution is obviously preferable to business that relies on capturing customers with "better" products. The definition of better has always changed with time, but this is an example of strategic policy-setting to redefine product benefits. The word *strategic* is vital because it encourages investment of personal ingenuity and energy for change. Now every Dutch employee in product manufacturing can potentially play a direct role in arriving at new solutions; it is no longer left to the regulator alone to define solutions.

- Regulation. Traditional regulations also play an important role in the new Dutch policy. Minimum performance standards on specific issues

(chemical emissions, energy consumption, etc.) are set by regulations; these standards will be combined with the new voluntary policy. Regulations cite LCA as the preferred method of defining environmental burdens, and regulations will be used to maintain an information review process that is verifiable and comprehensible.
- Voluntary LCA information. Today, producers of all product categories are requested to distribute LCA information about their products. Initially, the government will aggressively request that certain producers distribute LCA information as soon as possible. With time, more and more product categories will be targeted for LCA data distribution.
- Education. The Dutch government is educating the public on how to make an informed decision regarding environmental performance. These efforts include descriptions of environmental labeling, promotion of ecolabeling, establishment of an "independent information point," development of school education programs, and LCA-guided government procurement.

5.7.7 Communication

Improvement is the objective of the Dutch policy, and communication is seen as one of the most important accelerators. It is part of the regulations that communication must be based on an LCA approach. There are different kinds of communication:
- Information provided to purchasers along the supply cycle, linking raw material suppliers to end-product manufacturers.
- Information provided to end-product consumers at the point of sale. [*Editors' note*: At the time of the workshop, consumer education was included in the product policy; however, in November 1995, the emphasis shifted away from this goal because of the difficulty associated with defining an effective labeling system.]
- Information in the form of product "dossiers" detailing the environmental impact of end products. This information will serve to facilitate supervision and verification; it is also the basis for consumer information that is displayed on the product.
- Information and publicity, from the government to the public, generally is designed to raise the awareness in this field and to stimulate the use of information.

5.7.8 Summary

While the Dutch policy has only recently been implemented, it has attractive features. If successful in terms of environmental improvements, efficient and effective use of resources, and realized economic benefits, this approach may be applicable to other governments.

The question of applying the Dutch system to the U.S. system is interesting and challenging. U.S. industries have shown considerable interest in the Dutch system but not in additional regulation. The possibility of giving a company the option of demonstrating overall environmental improvements, LCA data, instead of complying with some of the existing regulations has possibilities. This would not obviate the need for minimum standards but would reduce the extensive reporting required by myriad regulations, in return for a company's producing an annual LCA database.

5.8 Barriers

Cutting across all applications of public policy and regulation are several common obstacles to the successful use of life-cycle concepts and approaches. The practitioners of LCA and those using data from LCAs have a responsibility to find solutions to these problems.

Common obstacles to applying life-cycle concepts in public policy include these:
- Lack of education
- Lack of acceptance of LCA concepts as decision-making tools
- Lack of stakeholder participation / partnerships
- Requirements for data confidentiality
- Difficulty in defining scope / boundaries
- Shortage of time and resources and inability to meet costs
- Lack of tools and data

5.8.1 Lack of education

Currently, knowledge of life-cycle concepts and approaches tends to be limited to a select few in the public policy arena. And although the number of technical and policy persons who are gaining information on and practicing LCA is growing, many key decision-makers are unfamiliar with the tool. For successful implementation, education of all who are involved with policy and regulatory decisions will be essential. This is true for both the government and private sectors. The values and limitations of LCA concepts and methodologies must be translated into common language that officials and decision-makers understand. Part of the educational message is that LCA can bring more data into a decision matrix, to allow for better policy and regulatory results. Successful case studies must be well advertised, to help educate all parties. This same sense of educational need is apparent for the public as well. To help build trust and credibility with the public stakeholder, practitioners of LCA need to provide education and effective communication.

5.8.2 Lack of acceptance of life-cycle concepts as decision-making tools

Tied closely to education is the acceptance of LCA as a decision-making tool. Two executives may discuss a magazine article that compares the use of paper versus plastic bags. While they understand it is a matter of assessing trade-offs, do they understand that an accepted LCA methodology must stand behind the decision? And what will be their reaction when a staff person comes to them, outlining a project that will use LCA as part of the decision-making process? Acceptance and support by those who have responsibility and control is essential.

To help build this acceptance and support, successful uses of LCA in policy and regulatory decisions need to be captured and highlighted. By example it can be shown how LCA benefited the process and, likewise, where LCA was not the best tool to use. As decision-makers come to accept life-cycle concepts, caution will also have to be exercised, acknowledging that these concepts cannot solve every problem. It goes directly back to identifying goals and assessing if LCA can effectively contribute.

5.8.3 Lack of stakeholder participation / partnerships

Throughout the review of LCA case studies, a common thread is the identification and involvement of the stakeholder. Case study reviews have shown that where there has been effective participation, buy-in, goal-setting, data collection, assessment, and implementation have been more successful. The use of a stakeholder partnership defines a sense of responsibility. This responsibility then translates into a need to work together to find a successful solution to the goal, providing a win / win situation. The traditional regulatory process has frequently resulted in a win / lose or a lose / lose situation, where it may not even be clear who the winners and losers are. For example, under the U.S. Toxic Substances Control Act (TSCA), all uses of a hazardous manufacturing chemical may be banned. Using LCA concepts in combination with other tools like risk assessment, however, USEPA may find that not all uses of the chemical pose a hazard.

Identifying the stakeholders and gaining their participation will not be easy for some policy issues. Time and care may need to be taken, particularly with more sensitive issues, to forge these partnerships. If there has historically been an adversarial relationship between stakeholders, the policy-maker must work to build bridges to gain effective participation. Trust and credibility must be established throughout the process, not only to define the goal but also to gather data, complete analysis, and communicate and implement the decision.

Integrating a variety of policy instruments within an issue can also effectively build the partnership. If instead of laying out a command-and-control structure as the goal, combining a voluntary program with financial incentives may result in a greater willingness by all parties to participate and succeed. To move public policy and regulatory decision-making forward, these new partnerships will be essential because they will encourage the examination of issues in a holistic manner.

5.8.4 Requirements for data confidentiality

Understanding the different aspects of the relationship or partnership could also help to identify solutions. This is particularly true of the obstacle of confidentiality. Whether it is getting information to those conducting the study, getting resulting information to those who will need to implement the decision, or getting information into the hands of the public, part of the challenge is to receive and handle data and information in an appropriate manner, respecting its possible sensitivity.

In many applications, industry data will be needed in the public policy decision-making matrix. These data may be confidential with respect to a manufacturing process or competitive aspect of the product. All stakeholders need to be sensitive to this and work together to find a workable solution to providing and sharing information that will work for all. If a solution is not found, trust is lost and the partnership deteriorates, therefore allowing the project to slip toward a lose / lose situation. One solution might be to consider a voluntary policy action that would not mandate the disclosure of certain detailed information but would still promote progress. Another could be to arrange for disclosure agreements and, by working through an accepted third party, to collect and aggregate data into a criteria average.

5.8.5 Difficulty in defining scope / boundaries

Once it has been determined that LCA or technical uncertainties might inform a policy decision, it is essential that the scope and boundaries of the study are well defined and that the uncertainties are clearly understood. The limitations of LCA concepts and methodologies are the primary drivers. A study might determine 30 different data points, under the auspices of needing a complete LCA, when for practical purposes of the decision at hand, 12 key or critical points would have provided sufficient information to feed into the decision process.

Careful planning is needed in this process because stakeholder participation is so critical to overcoming this obstacle. Each stakeholder brings to the table a different perspective on an issue. Developing consensus from the goal to the metrics can be extremely difficult. The nature of the process can lead to the development of an extensive laundry list of criteria. The challenge is to keep the group focused, to result in efficient and effective process definition. This can sometimes be accomplished by taking a stepped approach to the problem: applying the concept of "walk before you run" or having all the elements listed and then deciding which ones can or should be tackled first. Everyone has to acknowledge that there will always be some level of risk in the assumptions, but clear definition of scope and boundaries helps in the final communication and implementation.

5.8.6 Shortage of time and resources and inability to reduce costs

As with so many other decision-making tools, the available time, resources, budget, and associated costs can be major hurdles to overcome. Pressure is on to make key decisions in shorter time periods at less expense. The premise is that LCA can provide a better scientific foundation for some decisions; however, LCA is not necessarily the quickest, only, or best tool available. The consensus process needs to continue the development of concepts and methodologies to formulate efficient and effective applications of LCA. Budget and resource pressures can in part be eased by education and acceptance of the methodology. Not all organizations will be able to afford the incorporation of LCA. Small government agencies may not have the technical skills or finances available to hire consultants to conduct LCAs. There will need to be reliance on other data sources and entities to help these organizations in their applications. The reality of these constraints needs to be factored into the goal and scoping definition, if they cannot be overcome by other means.

5.8.7 Lack of tools and data

From a practical standpoint, complete LCAs are not yet ready for comprehensive application. The impact assessment phase is not finalized. Even those framework elements that are defined — goal definition and scoping, and inventory analysis — may not be readily adaptable into a format that every decision-maker can use. Tools need to be developed that will allow for all decision-makers, not just specialized LCA practitioners, to incorporate life-cycle concepts and methodologies. This relates in part to cost factors. A small company cannot afford to hire a consultant to conduct a comprehensive LCA for a new product design and to collect the data needed to conduct the LCA. However, if certain tools were available, the company's design engineer could review design considerations and make a choice that would lead to the environmental improvement of a product. Many aspects of life-cycle concepts and methodologies relate to tool availability. The range of topics is large, capturing general concept applications, inventories, more comprehensive applications, definition of weighting factors, and trade-offs. Data availability, applicability, and quality are also issues that need resolution for effective LCA application.

There is no one ideal solution to overcoming these common obstacles. The solutions, like the public policy goals themselves, are unique and are tied to the proposed life-cycle application.

5.9 LCA in strategic policy planning: international perspectives

Emerging international experiences with the use of LCA reveal that the tool can be valuable in strategic policy planning and as a vehicle for catalyzing broad-scale industrial improvements. In the United States, LCA is developing as a public policy tool through pilot applications that primarily involve assessing technological alternatives for research and development and for rulemaking. These pilot projects are intended to verify the usefulness of this tool for program and regulatory management. However, experiences in European nations and Japan indicate that LCA may also be an effective element of higher-level policy planning and a means of catalyzing broader-scale environmentally responsible behavior by industry and government.

In the European Community, LCA is being explored to determine the value of wastes and waste hierarchies for paper packaging. In the United States, federal policy defines a hierarchy of preferences for waste management processes: source reduction, reuse, recycling, incineration, and landfill. However, an LCA conducted in France indicates that adhering to this hierarchy will not always provide the optimal reduction of environmental impact and that exceptions to this hierarchy are warranted.

As a result of LCAs, a proposed European directive on packaging and packaging wastes, dated 21 Feb 1994 (Ecobalance 1994), requires that within five years, 50% to 65% of the weight of packaging wastes should be reused, recycled, incinerated, or composted. The directive further proposes that between 25% and 45% of the weight of packaging wastes should be recycled with a minimum of 15% for each packaging material (Ecobalance 1994). Although recycling is clearly given priority in this policy, it is also recognized that in some cases the more environmentally sound alternative may be to incinerate or landfill the packaging waste.

In Japan, the Ministry of International Trade and Industry recently published a report titled "Industrial Environmental Vision," which summarizes life-cycle profiles for 15 major industrial sectors (Tsusho Sangyo Sho 1994). The purpose of this analysis is to facilitate strategic policy planning by identifying potentially significant environmental improvements, needed technology development, and potential environmental markets. Industry-wide life-cycle profiles are thus being used by this economic ministry as a means of grasping the magnitude of the possibilities for improvement in important sectors of the economy.

A very intriguing use of LCA is being initiated by the government of the Netherlands. As described in Section 5.7, the government, with Parliament's concurrence, has asked all firms in the country to have independent LCAs conducted of their products. In conducting the LCAs, the firms can identify opportunities for improvement and can use the data generated by the LCA to advertise their environmental characteristics of their products. The government encourages consumers to consider the environmental characteristics of the products that they purchase, hoping to bring attention to the more environmentally sound products. Temptations to exaggerate data are countered by commercial competitors, who are free to challenge LCA claims, and by the government, which has the option to publish the corrected LCA data in the press. The Netherlands thus leverages the use of LCA by all firms to bring about an industry-wide improvement in environmental impacts.

In the United States, LCA is not yet used as a broad, policy planning tool. U.S. environmental policy has historically focused on health risk and not on material flows. Including material flow assessments with the use of LCA thus offers the

CHAPTER 5: POLICY AND REGULATIONS   103

potential for making new and substantial contributions to the formation of U.S. environmental policies.

Industry-wide, nationwide, life-cycle profiles as conducted in Japan can help U.S. policy-makers to identify and prioritize opportunities for environmental improvement. The use of LCA for establishing general policy guidelines, as in the European Community case, can help to more effectively guide materials and waste management. Finally, the promotion of LCA as an instrument for catalyzing in-house improvements, as in the Netherlands, may offer substantial potential in the U.S. as well. Although similar product requirements in the U.S. would be difficult to achieve, illustrating the value of LCA through its inclusion in high profile awards, such as the Malcolm Baldridge National Quality Award, and through its inclusion as a permitting requirement are possible steps to encourage widespread adoption.

International experiences with LCA illustrate how its benefits to the policy-maker and to the ultimate user may be leveraged to achieve broader benefits from this tool than from current approaches in the United States.

5.10 Observations and recommendations

5.10.1 Observations
The diversity of public policy and regulatory issues is such that there are many ways in which life-cycle concepts and methodologies can be applied. The objective and scope of the policy under consideration determine the life-cycle approach. The use of a stakeholder process is essential to determining if a life-cycle application will improve decision-making.

Life-cycle assessment has not been used in public policy applications as much as it has been used in some industrial applications that focus on product design. Within the public policy arena, there are many potential LCA applications because of the need to advance decision-making choices that will reduce environmental burdens, the need to take a broader view in identifying opportunities for environmental improvement, and the need to assess trade-offs between options.

5.10.2 Recommendations
While a foundation of LCA applications exists, it is recognized that the use of LCA in public policy is new and, as such, needs to be explored further. It should also be clearly noted that there is the potential for misusing LCA within the process of public policy decision-making. Therefore, LCA should always be used within the context of accepted principles and practices. The following recommendations highlight what are viewed as the most critical needs for effectively implementing LCA within public policy decision-making:

SETAC Press

- Continue to ensure that stakeholder involvement occurs early and throughout the process, regardless of the level or extent of the LCA application.
- Encourage strong partnerships among government, industry, and other stakeholders.
- Encourage the use of case studies and pilot testing of life-cycle concepts and applications, particularly as a strategic planning tool. Document and communicate case studies to demonstrate successful LCA applications and to identify drawbacks.
- Develop incentives for life-cycle concepts and LCA to be applied by governments and industries.
- Encourage governments and public entities to learn from the industry's experience with LCA applications.
- Develop a practical and acceptable impact assessment component for more effective use of LCA in public policy.
- Ensure that all who are involved with and control public policy are educated on the use of life-cycle concepts and applications.

5.11 References

Dutch Ministry of Housing, Spatial Planning, and the Environment. 1994. Policy document on products and the environment. The Hague, Netherlands (PO Box 20951, 2500 EZ The Hague). VROM 94196/h/5094 13042/168.

Ecobalance Inc. 1994. Translation of some abstracts of the European directive on packaging and packaging wastes (February 21, 1994). Wayne NJ: Ecobalance Inc.

Shapiro K, Little R, White A. 1993. Incorporation of life-cycle assessment concepts in rulemaking procedures: a discussion paper. Report to USEPA Office of Pollution Prevention and Toxics (OPPT). Boston: Tellus Institute.

Tsusho Sangyo Sho, Sangyo Kozo Shingikai Chikuy Kankyobukai. 6 Jun 1994. Sangyo kankyo bishion.

[USEPA] U.S. Environmental Protection Agency. 1989. Preliminary data summary for industrial laundries. Washington DC: USEPA Office of Water. EPA 440/1-89/103.

Chapter 6
Environmental Technology

6.1 Introduction

6.1.1 Overview: technology, public policy, and life-cycle concepts

The connections between life-cycle concepts, public policy, and technology are complex and tightly interwoven. This chapter attempts to unravel those connections in order to assess the potential of life-cycle concepts as public policy design tools and as public policy components. This chapter follows a construction built on the following premises:

- The present ways in which technologies come to life and are put into practice are inadequate to satisfy environmental concerns.
- New forms of public policies (and other sets of guiding principles) are needed to promote the innovation, adoption, and use of technologies that better reflect what are deemed to be environmental norms, i.e., what the environment would tell us are the right things to do, if the environment could speak authoritatively.
- Life-cycle approaches are useful tools, methodologies, and principles to help formulate appropriate public policies and to implement the policies at all levels along the product life cycle.
- The innovation, adoption, and use of appropriate environmental technologies is manifest in several temporal and institutional contexts; each separate context requires different policies and applications of LCA.

6.1.2 Definitions

Technology has been characterized as both the primary cause of environmental degradation and its most promising savior. Technology, through its form and function, translates human needs and demands into useful hardware, software, systems, and services.

Environmental technology is an evolutionary hybrid, defined simply as any technology that advances the environmental compatibility of products and services according to marketplace and public policy norms and by applicable cultural and institutional norms.

In the context of economic activity, environmental compatibility has been captured in the concept of sustainable development, which refers to the viability of natural resources and ecosystems under the pressures exerted by economic growth. For the purposes of this chapter, environmental compatibility may be enhanced through the development, deployment, and commercialization of technology that has the net result of combining improved cost effectiveness, and therefore economic viability, with

- improved energy efficiency, and/or
- reduced consumption of natural resources, and/or
- reduced environmental releases and thereby reduced impact on global and/or
- regional infrastructure as it relates to human and ecosystem health over the complete life cycle of the product or service (i.e., raw material acquisition through manufacturing, distribution, use/reuse, and ultimate disposition).

6.1.3 Relationship of technology to public policy

Technology development has several drivers. In the industrial arena, innovative forces have been oriented toward the creation of the "better mousetrap" with the inherent goal of meeting consumer needs, expanding market share, and therefore improving the financial health of an enterprise. Further efforts have been directed at improvements in quality that translate customer needs into refined production processes and systems that seek to eliminate waste while consistently delivering a highly defined product or service.

In the public arena, technology development has focused on the delivery of systems that respond to issues such as national defense or on the pursuit of knowledge through scientific research that would support the industrial competitiveness of a nation.

Changes in the political landscape (i.e., the end of the Cold War and the evolution of the global marketplace) coupled with a growing concern for the preservation of the natural environment have presented policy-makers with an unprecedented opportunity to redeploy significant resources toward the development of environmental technology.

In essence, public policy may now be crafted to create technologies that satisfy the needs of a new customer, the natural environment, in addition to meeting the needs of human society. If the "customer" and producer have perfect information then only the right technologies, that is those that were "right" according to some idea of environmental norms, would survive in a competitive market.

6.1.4 Relationship of LCA to public policy

Both the public and private sectors listen to a host of institutional speakers when they establish policy and take action. In recent years, environmental advocates and other concerned NGOs have begun to exert powerful forces on strategic and operational decision-making. Science, as an institutional sector, has much to say about the limits of the environment to satisfy all human demands over a foreseeable time frame. Industrial sector groups, such as the Chemical Manufacturers' Association in the U.S. and similar groups in Europe, are instrumental in creating broad codes of management practices that introduce environment into technology.

All sectors are important, and all come into play at different times and through different routes into the public- and private-sector action-producing structures. Life-cycle concepts can and should play a role in informing these voices within and without a sector as to how to make the technological choice reflect the concerns (demands) of the environment as well as the demands of society.

Public policy can address multiple stakeholders as well; some public policy directly informs (and thereby influences) consumer choice and indirectly causes companies to expand their output of environmental technologies. Labeling and other information-giving policies fall into this category. The potential role of life-cycle concepts in these arenas is obvious and is discussed in detail in Chapter 3.

Public policy can be directed at a firm itself, in many forms, again informed by and containing applications of life-cycle concepts. The whole notion of extended producer responsibility is a notion that is designed to make a firm responsible for managing its products over the life cycle with the expectation that it will then make the products better in some way. The current thrust is to close the post-consumer end of the product life cycle. It is arguable that life-cycle concepts were used to design this policy, but it is clear that the policy represents life-cycle thinking.

For the government, life-cycle concepts can be used to rationalize the distortions that have entered policy and regulatory frameworks by failures to design these policies in a holistic, life-cycle context. What has transpired is the consequence of limited knowledge, other more senior policies, and political realities. To the extent that current political reality looks to such rationalization, LCA can be a powerful tool at the conceptual or macro level and as an analytic methodology to assist in sorting out priorities and options (always a daunting task in a complex society).

Public policy may be manifest in a variety of instruments. Traditional policy vehicles include regulatory and fiscal dimensions, while the emerging trends are shifting toward market-based stimuli and the formation of voluntary initiatives. The full continuum of these vehicles may be employed in the creation of effective policy to support environmental technologies and can be effectively supported by the application of life-cycle concepts. Creating a balance of regulation, economic instruments, and voluntary initiatives is widely recognized as a most promising approach.

6.1.5 Using LCA in policy to promote environmental technology

With this preamble, how should life-cycle concepts be more directly tied to the evolution and proliferation of environmental technologies? It may be helpful to address this question by looking at different time horizons, as the roles of the institutional players change with respect to the horizon in which technological change is being focused.

Short-term innovation: market forces dominate, consumer choice is primary. In the short term, market forces are the most effective agent of change. For example, changes in purchasing patterns can increase the relative amount of environmental technology in use and can send a signal to producers to bring more of these types of goods and services to the marketplace. An informed consumer and purchasing agent can pick, from the set of existing technologies, those that can be discerned as "better" than others according to some "environmental criteria." Life-cycle concepts can help form these criteria, but in and of itself, the notion of life cycle is not such a criterion; it is a framework for the development of criteria. The normative part of "better" has to come from some legitimate social voice. Hopefully, the environment will be better served if life-cycle frameworks are used. This specific application is addressed more thoroughly in Chapters 3 and 4.

Intermediate-term innovation: company research in product design, process improvement and substitution are key. The next level of technologies are likely to come from the current structures in producer sectors. For example, educated consumers who understand the life-cycle implications of their purchases and use of products and services can change their buying preferences which will, in turn, affect market demand and be reflected in companies' responses. Designers can be given new design tools, based on life-cycle principles, to satisfy these new concerns. Public policy can act to produce public education with a life-cycle context. Companies can be assisted in moving their resources to proactive environmental practices that focus on innovative environmental technologies by relieving them of overly burdensome and ineffective regulatory requirements. Integrated permits and regulations based on life-cycle frameworks can support such a rationalization.

Long-term innovation: company strategy, social and functional innovation, supra-company institutions are essential. The next and possibly most encompassing technology innovation will transcend organization boundaries. For example, networks or centers of excellence, which bring together related industries and other institutional sectors, will evaluate complete product systems and look for synergistic opportunities to achieve environmental goals. Public policy can use life-cycle thinking to formulate strategies that stimulate the formation of such compatible clusters.

6.1.6 Integration framework

Environmental policy reflects the need to supplement the everyday practices of societies with guides, principles, information, and other means for introducing environmental concerns into every phase of public and private life. Traditional forms of public policy have been extraordinarily effective in reducing the mass of harmful substances flowing into the environment and the amounts of waste produced and given to the environment. At the same time, the existing framework of

Chapter 6: Environmental Technology

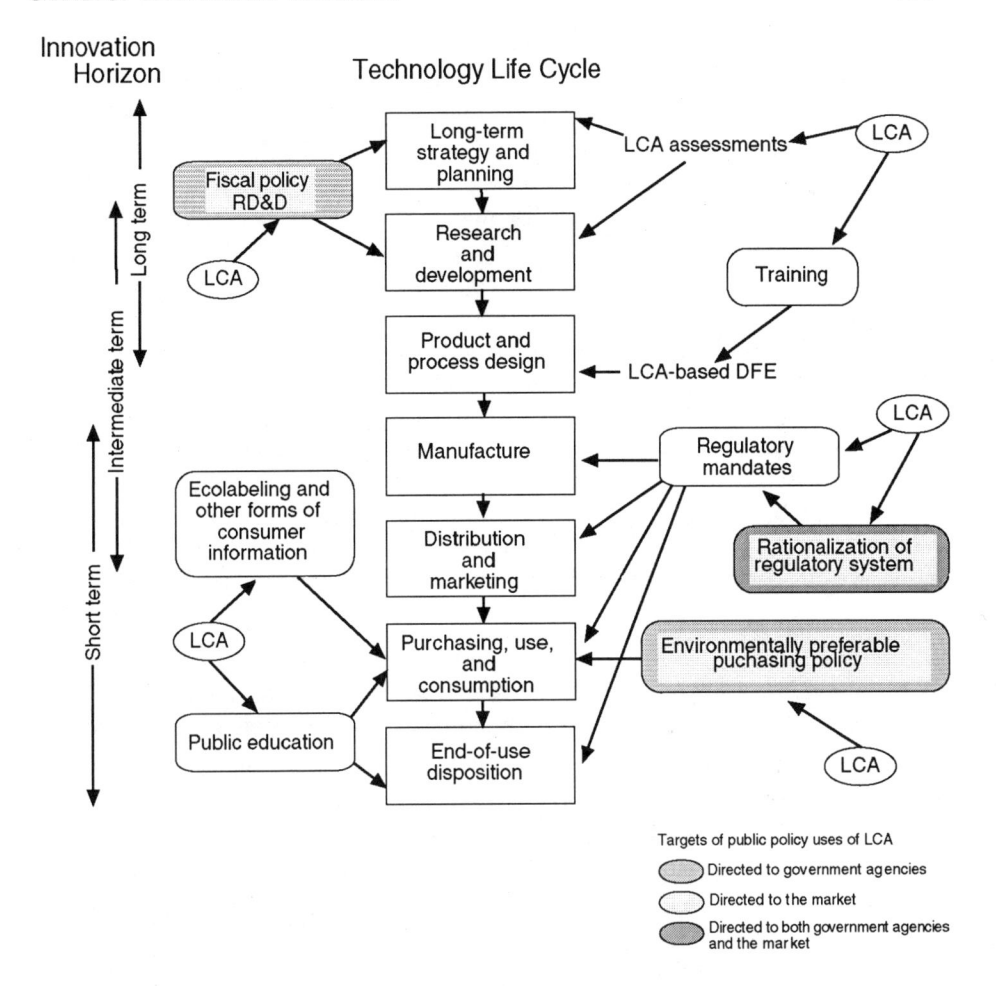

Figure 6-1   Integration framework: technology, public policy, LCA

policies lacks a coherent, holistic structure that reflects the impacts along the life cycle of all the goods and services that comprise the economy.

As outlined above, life-cycle concepts offer a powerful way to improve the effectiveness of policy-making and of the policies themselves. The opportunities for use of life-cycle concepts in the policy process are manifold and need to be tailored to those areas where the policy intersects with the various stages of the technology life-cycle: product or process evolution (strategy/RD&D/design) through manufacturing, purchasing/use, and disposition. Figure 6-1 depicts the framework by which products and services are created and brought to the marketplace and illustrates points where different policies can be brought to bear. In many cases, LCA can provide the coherent and holistic inputs necessary to support the development of those policies.

SETAC Press

In Figure 6-1, the backbone represents the flow of activities that typify the technological life cycle of all types of goods and services, whether they are produced and/or used by government or private sector. Conceptually, this backbone is illustrated as a linear process. In its real-life application, it is a dynamic and highly iterative process. At the top are the long-range, strategic, or planning activities that shape the actions that occur in the parts of the path that follow below. Strategic decisions are followed by research, development, and demonstration, out of which a small set of potentially market-bound goods and services is selected. These winners are designed to become the new products and services and the manufacturing and logistic systems by which they are made and delivered. For goods, the manufacturing step is followed by marketing and distribution, by purchase and use, and finally by disposition. Knowledge gleaned from the downstream activities, combined with shifts in consumer and environmental demands are captured by the upstream activities to create the next generation of products and services. At most stages, public policy can be used to alter current and traditional modes of acting to introduce more environmentally beneficial outcomes.

The time delay between the stages and their effect on the environment decreases as one moves away from the strategic end (shown along the top of Figure 6-1). Policies that affect buying and use decisions will act more quickly to shift the environmental consequences of economic activities than will policies that guide the allocation of long-term research and development (R&D) funds by either companies or government agencies.

On either side are typical policy vehicles that can influence actions along the chain. At the top, government economic policies that serve to determine the allocation of research expenditures or influence similar private decisions (e.g., tax policy concerning the expending of research costs) will affect the whole process. Use of life-cycle concepts in assessing the potential products and services should lead to decisions that are better from an environmental point of view than those they are replacing and should ensure that entirely new goods and services do not carry any environmental surprises.

Traditional regulations apply more frequently to the manufacturing, marketing, and distribution part of the chain, including restrictions on the way manufacturing wastes can be treated. Life-cycle concepts can be used to guide the development of public policy at both the statutory and, more particularly, the regulatory levels. Initiatives at the USEPA such as the Common Sense initiative, aim at rationalizing the overall regulatory maze. This initiative reflects the need to bring a coherence to the whole body of regulations and consequent practices, which have evolved in a chaotic and particularistic manner without a framework that reflects the interconnectedness of environmental compartments and the life cycle

Chapter 6: Environmental Technology

of goods and services. Life-cycle assessments are essential tools in this and other related exercises.

Training professionals in the art of design for the environment based on life-cycle concepts should lead to specific products and processes that, again, are better than the ones they supersede. Environmentally preferable purchasing policy for federal, state, and local agencies, (e.g., as required in the recent Executive Order 12873 (1993) may directly influence choice and send strong signals to all those involved in the design, manufacture, and disposal of those products. Life-cycle concepts can and should be used to determine what product attributes may be used to select preferable products in any given class.

Nearer to the bottom of Figure 6-1 are policies that can influence patterns of consumption (and production) in the short term. Information-providing policies such as the Toxics Release Inventory (under the Superfund Amendments and Reauthorization Act [SARA]) or ecolabels and other product information should enable individual and institutional purchasers to make more informed environmental choices. These choices in turn will send signals to the producers that they should expand their offering of more environmentally preferable goods and services. Closely related to information-giving are policies that promote public understanding of the life-cycle consequences of their economic activities, and, as a consequence, better choices.

Section 6.2 provides a framework for public policy applications of life-cycle concepts and life-cycle assessments. Section 6.3 discusses general issues associated with using life-cycle assessments in public policy, and Section 6.4 provides an examination of recently conducted life-cycle assessments.

6.2 A framework for the use of life-cycle concepts in public policy

6.2.1 Introduction: some policy considerations and principles

In considering how to devise public policy using life-cycle considerations and how to execute policies using life-cycle tools that will drive environmental technology, we need to be informed by (and learn from) past experiences and current trends in policy development. These insights are noted below:

1) The trend toward complexity of materials used in product design is likely to make environmental evaluation of those products more difficult and expensive.

2) There are at least two alternative or concurrent design strategies that can be pursued in an environmental technology and life-cycle context:

   a) product-oriented design, which seeks to optimize the environmental attributes of a product within the constraints of the existing production/

SETAC Press

consumption system (usually accomplished within an individual company).
  b) systems-oriented design, which broadens the scope of optimization to include the changes in the production/consumption system itself, in addition to product design (accomplished through cooperative relationships among suppliers, manufacturers, and other actors like waste management providers).
3) There are always likely to be design trade-offs among alternative environmental attributes of a product system. (This highlights the need to employ analytical tools that account for the environmental costs and benefits of alternative design choices early in the design process.)
4) There is a tendency to focus on the most visible environmental issue/impact, even if it is not the most important, for example, state laws that effectively ban the purposeful introduction of heavy metals into packaging even though packaging is a relatively minor source of heavy metals in landfills and incinerators.
5) Life-cycle concepts take a broad perspective that considers all phases of the technology development process.
6) Life-cycle concepts may be employed to optimize the mix of control, remediation, and avoidance/prevention technologies employed in delivering a product or in configuring a production/consumption system.
7) The environmental consequences of product manufacture, distribution, use, and disposal tend to be multi-dimensional, impacting more than one environmental medium.

6.2.2 Research, development, and demonstration policy

Research, development, and demonstration policies direct public-sector financial, intellectual, and laboratory resources toward the pursuit of strategic public goals (national security, public health, energy independence, industrial competitiveness, and environmental protection). These resources serve to leverage or stimulate technology development by universities and private companies. In its recent document outlining the Clinton Administration's effort to advance environmental technologies (Technology for a Sustainable Future), the U.S. National Science and Technology Council (NSTC 1994) notes that "the government's role in encouraging environmental technologies has been underdeveloped." In the U.S., direct public-sector (including both state and federal) investments account for less than 10 percent of total expenditures on environmental technology innovation.

In Technology for a Sustainable Future, the NSTC has articulated strategies for fostering RD&D to advance environmental technologies. Given the relatively early state of strategy implementation, now is an opportune moment to incorporate life-cycle considerations into key RD&D agendas (civilian, energy, defense, environmental protection).

Historically, the environmental consequences of federal technology development has tended to be given minor consideration, although this is changing. For example, defense R&D, while maintaining its focus on strategic national defense objectives, has begun to incorporate life-cycle concepts. The U.S. DoD now requires environmental life-cycle costing as part of the agency's acquisitions process. This may serve as an appropriate model for infusing environmental life-cycle thinking and analysis into other key RD&D agendas.

6.2.3 Regulatory policy (U.S.)

Regulatory policies have been used to protect environmental quality by limiting the releases of pollutants and waste materials. In effect, these polices have changed the environmental attributes of products by raising the cost of releasing wastes into the air, water, or land (as in the case of the Clean Air Act, CWA and RCRA) and by directly controlling or limiting the use of certain chemicals and substances (as in the case of TSCA or FIFRA). Regulatory policies like the Toxics Release Inventory have, by design or by result, also led to changes in production by influencing public perceptions of a manufacturer's environmental "friendliness."

Regulatory policies regarding environmental protection have tended to be wastestream- or media-specific. They are usually manifested as standards that are based on currently available technologies. These standards have focused on end-of-pipe controls. Rarely have they emphasized prevention or avoidance of waste production and/or inefficient materials use. Compliance with each media standard (or set of standards) is treated as mutually exclusive from the next media and its standard (or set of standards). This regime of policies has provided little incentive for technological innovation and/or standards exceedance.

Recent developments in the U.S. and Europe provide models for incorporating life-cycle techniques into environmental policy development and implementation. Laws requiring companies to prepare individual facility plans, which account for the multi-media environmental impacts emanating from the facility in question, have been passed in approximately 17 states. In Europe, government regulations are holding manufacturers responsible for the environmental fate of their products. Such rules are likely to motivate re-design of producer/consumer systems.

6.2.4 Market stimulus (market-based) policies

This class of policies attempts to internalize costs (to producers and consumers) that were hitherto externalized. The intended effect is to provide price signals to manufacturers and consumers that motivate them to alter their production/consumption practices in ways that avoid/minimize waste discharges, disposal costs,

and/or materials use. Examples of market-based rules that have been implemented include these:
- Tradeable pollution permits
- Product taxes
- Deposit/refund laws
- Variable-rate pricing of solid-waste disposal services

Generally speaking, these rules have taken a media- or product-specific approach. Other market stimulus policies that have a high potential for inducing system-oriented (as opposed to product-oriented) optimization have been proposed or are under development, including the following:
- Elimination of subsidies and/or special tax treatment for virgin materials
- Voluntary agreements
- ISO standards

6.2.5 Fiscal policy

Public fiscal policy can support environmental technology through tax policies and public–private partnerships that encourage private sector investment. The U.S., far behind Japan and other G-7 countries in the percentage of gross domestic product invested in new plants and equipment, is not providing significant support to environmental technology. Tax credits for investment in environmental technology can be provided. Specific public–private partnerships can further environmental technology using existing mechanisms.

6.2.6 International commerce & foreign aid

The export of environmental technologies through either international commerce or foreign aid serves multiple purposes. The most obvious impact of providing technological advancement is that it minimizes impacts on the environment. In addition, it can provide a competitive advantage over other technologies.

There are a variety of existing organizations, e.g., the U.S. Department of Commerce, the National Trade Data Bank, and the U.S. Department of Energy, utilizing technologies abroad that can lead to investment from foreign governments. U.S. aid similarly demonstrates U.S. technology and offers a good opportunity to demonstrate the advantages of environmental technology to countries undergoing economic development.

It would be beneficial for future technology export to demonstrate environmental technologies that will provide the greatest environmental protection and efficiency possible. Long-term growth for U.S. industry may depend on the acknowledged superiority of the environmental technology the U.S. can demonstrate in the foreign markets.

SETAC Press

6.2.7 Education and training

Education and training are critical components of public policy and are directly related to the successful development of environmental technologies. Education and training not only create the capability to develop environmental technologies but also increase the general population's appreciation for ecological issues and the advantages of LCA.

In the U.S., educational and training opportunities are limited to a relatively small number of teaching institutions. USEPA's National Advisory Council on Environmental Policy and Technology found that 10 to 15 of the nearly 400 engineering schools and 25 of the 700 business schools offered a significant amount of coursework on waste prevention (Cortese 1992).

LCA is not cited as a prominent feature of the curricula at the 13 U.S. universities noted in Green Products by Design: Choices for a Cleaner Environment (U.S. Congress 1992).

In contrast, Sweden will open its National Center for Excellence for Life-Cycle Assessment in Gothenberg in January 1995. The Center will be a focal point for the advancement of LCA and will serve as the national training facility. Representatives from industry as well as graduate and undergraduate students from various disciplines will attend the center. Funding will be provided equally by industry and the government. The center will develop teachers as well as those applying LCA as part of industry.

While dedicated educational efforts can accelerate the level of sophistication incorporated into LCA, more widespread educational initiatives are needed to assure success in the long term. Not only will widely available training encourage a larger number of practitioners, it will also create a larger group of knowledgeable people who will ultimately be consumers of these new technologies. The ultimate impact of public policy will be to foster a cultural shift in the population as a whole, so consumers grow to expect environmental technology products or services that progressively incorporate LCA more and more effectively. To accomplish this in the long term, understanding of environmental technology and LCA will need to be incorporated into all levels of our educational system.

6.2.8 Information dissemination

Public policy can encourage information dissemination by directly requiring federal agencies to supply information or by funding other institutions to do so. Expectations for various ecologically compatible products or services can be created by those efforts, especially when complemented by a broad-based educational effort.

Information exchanges among organizations involved in environmental technology can also be fostered by providing leadership, funding, or information exchange mechanisms that are not inhibited by regulations. A major issue for industry remains, however, regarding the protection of intellectual property.

Broad-based informational strategies can help educate consumers to be more receptive to environmental technology-produced products or services. They can also improve consumers' capability to differentiate between differing claims made by producers. Various organizations within the U.S. are presently initiating activities to communicate relative ratings for production methods that are less harmful ecologically than others. These organizations operate independently and are not government supported or sanctioned.

6.3 Life-cycle applications to public policy for environmental technology

LCAs can come in many different forms, depending on the goal of the study, but three broad categories emerge, each tailored for a specific use. The categories of LCAs are these:
- Rhetorical, informational, or claims-making
- Regulative or possibility-constraining
- Constitutive, consciousness-building, or possibility-creating

The categories tend to locate themselves along the technology life cycle (Figure 6-1) with the rhetorical type at the downstream activities and the regulative and the constitutive toward the upstream. These use categories pertain to the function of the LCA, not necessarily to the level of detail.

Rhetorical, informational, or claims-making. In this use category, LCAs are used to forward an argument that the product or other item being considered meets criteria. Usually, the type of LCA employed is the traditional form involving multiple data categories over the spectrum of life-cycle stages (i.e., cradle-to-grave).

Here the LCA is no different than any other "truth" claim made in a conversation among individuals or in writing about the object under consideration. Its truth is limited by the objective knowledge available and the boundaries of the framework. Some forms of ecolabeling and other product information fall into this category.

The history of risk assessment/risk management suggests the difficulties of making convincing claims. In many ways, risk makes a similar distinction when used in a claims-making or rhetorical setting. Rhetoric in this sense refers to its original meaning as a mode of argument among parties attempting to establish their position as superior. Much theory and practical experience shows that consideration of truth claims is always accompanied by assessment of the legitimacy and truthfulness (trustworthiness) of the party making the claim. These factors are critical in institutionalizing the use of LCAs as claims-making tools.

Chapter 6: Environmental Technology

Regulative or possibility-constraining. LCAs can and have been used as regulative devices. In this application, the output of an LCA is used to restruct the activity being contemplated. These LCAs usually employ a narrow band of data categories or concentrate on specific life-cycle stages that have been established as the dominant stages with respect to the objective or purpose of the study.

Proposed mandated use of LCAs to determine what is an environmentally preferable product is one example. The output of this LCA would draw a boundary around one group of acceptable products, leaving out all the rest. Ecolabels fall somewhere in between this category and the first one depending on the authority behind them. If the label is merely indicative of the performance, then it is a rhetorical device. If the label is used to restrict entry to the market or consumer preferences, then it becomes regulative.

This use of LCAs may have the effect of constraining innovation as it sets up a target for the designers, which they will try to meet along with all the other design goals. If the LCA is broad and accurately maps environmental needs into the framework, then the products of innovation will approach the framers' goals. If, as is so often the case, the LCA framework is limited by knowledge and practical boundaries, then innovative process may more closely resemble a contest over which designer earns the best score.

Constitutive, consciousness-building, or possibility-creating. The constitutive category of LCA corresponds to the conceptual level of LCA use. Here, the goal is to open up the awareness of those involved in planning, design, decision-making, and other cognitive activities to a world beyond that to which they have grown accustomed. The studies employ qualitative or semiquantitative analysis. The main focus is to highlight where further detailed analysis will be focused once the strategic options have been selected.

Again, there is much theory and practical experience that attests to the power of systems that can break up and re-create the mental models on which humans act. This is the heart of much of the success of total quality management (TQM).

Constitutive means that LCA contributes to the constitution or creation of new modes of thought and to new modes of action that flow from the thinking process. This mode is of particular interest in the design stages along the technology life cycle, for it is in the design process that new possibilities are opened up in the form of new products, processes, organizational forms, and means of communication and coordination. This application is also important in policy formulation where much environmental policy has emerged from the regulative mode. Here, LCAs can be powerful tools for opening up the innovative powers of individuals and organizations to these new worlds.

LCA-based DFE tools may bridge the regulative and constitutive categories. The use of matrices and checklists that have been created by an LCA consciousness-raising process generally contain items that both restrain the designer to certain environmentally sound practices and encourage the designer to consider a broader domain of options.

6.4 Life-cycle applications in public policy development

6.4.1 Study introduction and purpose

In order to assess the current status of the use of LCA in public policy, particularly with respect to the spectra of LCA uses and the stakeholders involved, a cursory analysis of international case studies was performed (Table 6-1). The purpose of this analysis was to assess current trends and to suggest future directions of LCA applications to public policy.

Three variables were examined for each study. The first variable appraised was the degree of technological innovation represented by the product system examined in the LCA. The distinctions in technological innovation were discussed above (Section 6.1.5); their range includes short-term innovations focused on existing products, where market forces and consumer choices are paramount; intermediate-term innovations more oriented toward product or process design changes, including both improvements and substitutions among products; and long-term innovations representing revolutionary new company or supra-company strategies with the potential to abruptly alter or replace entire technology categories.

The second variable examined for each study was its relative position on the LCA spectrum of uses and approaches discussed in Section 6.2.1. This spectrum generally extended from rhetorical or claims-making applications, in which the conventional, highly quantitative and data-intensive approach used by early LCA practitioners was relevant, to more conceptual and qualitative applications. This variable, as with the level of technological innovation, was subjective in nature and was judged on a relative basis considering all of the studies collectively.

The third variable considered in this analysis was the category of public policy to which the study was directed. Seven categories of public policy were considered: 1) research, development, and demonstration policies; 2) regulatory policy; 3) market stimulus policy; 4) fiscal policy; 5) international commerce and foreign aid; 6) education and training policy; and 7) information dissemination policy. For most studies, both the primary and secondary policy orientations were identified

6.4.2 Case studies examined

The analysis examined 24 LCA studies sponsored by North American, Western European, and Japanese government agencies. Only government-sponsored studies were included in this analysis due to their direct application to, or expression

Table 6-1 Public sector LCA studies

Study number, country, year	Agency, [contractor]	Description	Purpose
1) Sweden 1994	Swedish Environment Protection Agency [AF-IPK]	Calculations of environmental consequences of ecocycle bill; LCA of packages (in Swedish)	Evaluate environmental consequences following suggested levels for material reuse and recycling according to ecocycle bill
2) Sweden 1992	Swedish National Board for Industrial and Technical Development, Vattenfall AB, Swedish EPA	Life of fuels: motor fuels from source to end use	Compare different potential systems for production of fuel ethanol, including comparison with other fuel alternatives
3) Sweden 1995	Swedish National Board for Road Administration [Institute for Environmental Research]	LCA of roads: a model study (in Swedish) (IVL report B1210)	LCI conducted on infrastructures, especially construction and maintenance of roads; intent is to introduce LCA as tool for improvement of long-term decisions
4) U.S. 1992	Department of Energy (DOE)	Electric car LCA	Determine effects of mandating use of zero-emission electric vehicles
5) U.S. 1993	Department of Energy (DOE)	Total Energy Cycle Assessment	Cradle-to-grave analysis of different energy options, including renewables
6) U.S. 1974	Environmental Protection Agency (USEPA) [MRI]	Comparative LCA of beverage containers	
7) U.S. 1991	Council of State Governments [Tellus]	LCA of packaging materials alternatives	
8) U.S. 1978	Environmental Protection Agency (USEPA) [MRI]	Study of milk containers	
9) U.S. 1993	Department of Defense (DoD)	Weapons design for lessening environmental impacts of weapons disposal	Get new weapon systems designers to factor in environmentally benign disposal methods at end of useful life
10) Europe Union Comm. 1992		Ecolabeling	

Table 6-1 continued

Study number, country, year	Agency [contractor]	Description	Purpose
11) U.S. 1994	Environmental Protection Agency (USEPA)	Industrial laundries effluent guidelines and standards	
12) U.S. 1994	Department of Energy (DOE)	Biomass-ethanol	Compare life-cycle emissions of gasoline from petroleum feedstocks vs ethanol from agricultural feedstocks for transportation fuel
13) France 1993	(ADEM)	Analysis of waste management options in order to prepare French position on European directive relative to packaging and packaging waste	
14) U.S., in progress	EPA	Options analysis of hazardous solid waste combustion	
15) The Netherlands, in progress	Dutch government product and environmental program	LCA for ecolabeling	
16) U.S., in progress	Environmental Protection Agency (USEPA) [RTI]	Comparison of municipal solid waste (MSW) management options	
17) Japan, in progress	MITI	Inventory of major industries (aluminum, steel, paper, utilities, textiles, etc.)	
18) Canada 1994	Environment Canada	Options analysis of environment profiles of packaging systems	
19) Canada 1994	Environment Canada	Raw material database project	
20) U.S., in progress	Environmental Protection Agency (USEPA) [Batelle]	Carpeting system LCA	
21) Sweden 1994	Swedish EPA/ Forest industry [Institute for Environmental Research]	Ecocycles and paper packages: material recycling or energy recovery (in Swedish), (IVL Report E1128). LCA on waste paper from packaging	Compare material reuse and energy recovering of waste paper from packaging with respect to resource consumption, environmental impact, and cost

Table 6-1   continued

Study number, country, year	Agency, [contractor]	Description	Purpose
22) Austria 1993	International Institute for Applied Systems Analysis	LCA on large-scale recycling of paper	Broaden debate about material reuse contra energy recovery
23) Germany 1993	Fraunhofer Institute	LCA on different types of paper containers, reusable glass bottles, and plastic bottles	Evaluate correlation between environmental impact, transportation, and number of times that beverage packages can be used
24) Sweden 1994	Swedish EPA [Chalmers University, Institute for Environmental Research]	LCA on paper beverages	Investigate difference in results that might occur from different data input; parallel to study 1 in this table

of, public policies. Time constraints within this workshop also restricted the scope of the analysis. This is not to say that privately sponsored studies do not have the capacity to influence public policy; indeed, a comparative analysis of government and private studies according to these variables would be extremely interesting and highly illuminating. For purposes of this cursory analysis, however, the trends evident from the government-sponsored studies alone can provide helpful guidance to future LCA development.

6.4.3 Results and discussion

The relationships of the 24 case studies were plotted according to the level of technological innovation of the product system analyzed and the type of LCA conducted (Figure 6-2). The majority of studies (18 of the 24) are clustered in a relatively narrow domain representing LCAs that are descriptive in nature and that address product systems of short- to intermediate-term technological innovation.

The nature of the majority of the studies examined is highly quantitative and detailed. Fewer studies have employed an abbreviated LCA format, focusing on a selected number of emissions or resource parameters deemed to represent the most important aspects of the product systems studied.

The short- to intermediate-term technological innovations largely reflect studies of existing products and comparative product LCAs, and studies of alternative product or process technology design. Only four of the studies examined addressed product systems representing a high level of technological innovation.

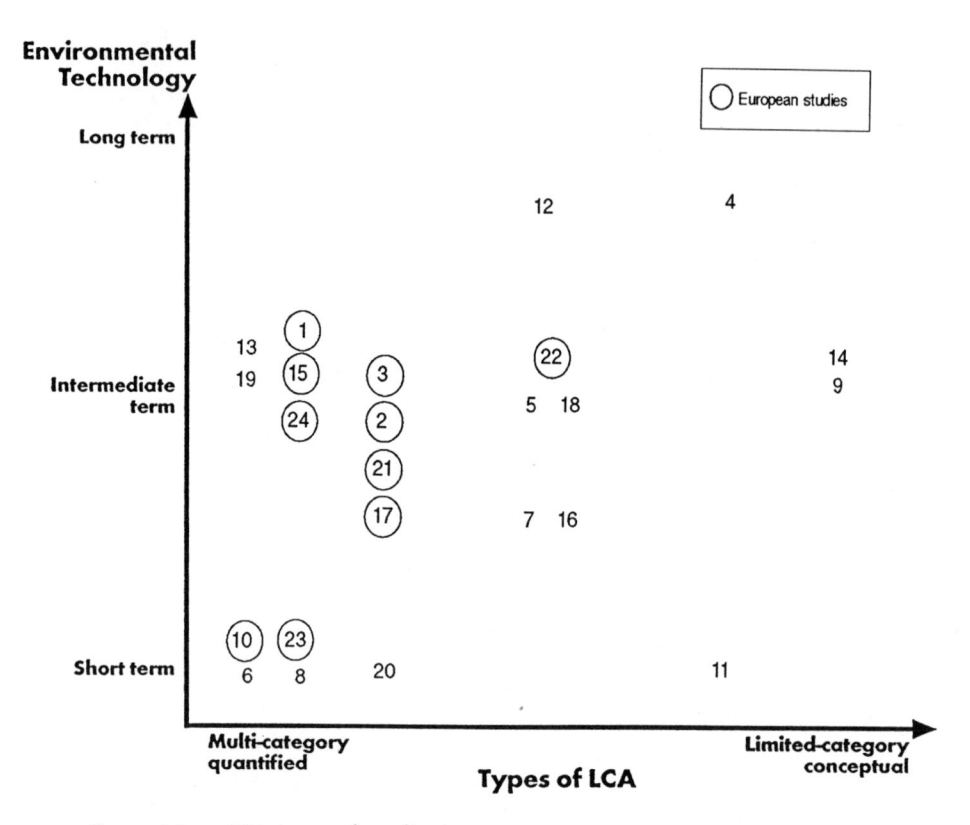

Figure 6-2   LCA type and application

Two of the studies (numbers 4 and 12) are studies by U.S. DOE of biomass-to-ethanol conversion and of electric vehicles. Application of LCA toward higher level technological innovation clearly represents a potentially valuable application of future LCA methodology. Similarly, only 4 of the 24 studies examined could be classified as conceptual in nature. A conceptual approach was employed in the DOE study (number 4) of electric vehicles, in two USEPA studies (numbers 11 and 14) to determine effluent guidelines for ILs and to compare hazardous solid-waste combustion alternatives, and in a U.S. DoD study (number 9) of weapons disposal systems. The increasing emphasis on pollution prevention, DFE, and other environmental management strategies is likely to lead to increasing conceptual use of LCA.

CHAPTER 6: ENVIRONMENTAL TECHNOLOGY   123

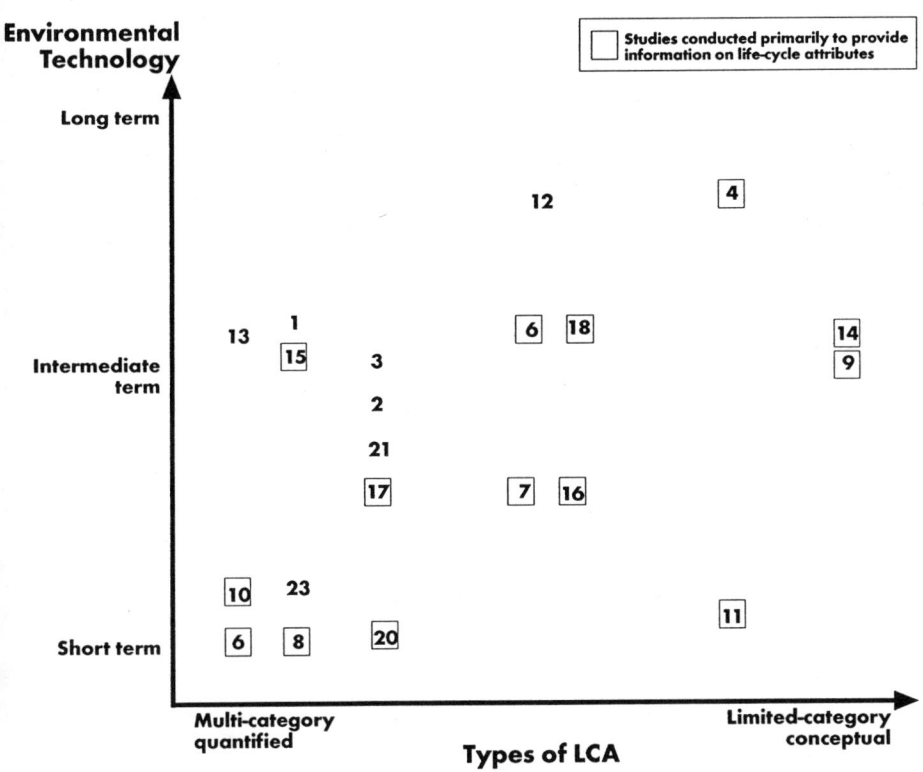

Figure 6-3   Information dissemination orientation

6.4.4 LCA as a tool in forming environmental public policy

The 24 LCA studies examined (Figure 6-2) were further distinguished into general areas of public policy orientation reflecting the primary purpose for which they were conducted. The 24 studies were distributed along four key public policy orientations: information dissemination, research and development, market stimulation, and regulatory.

Information dissemination. Those studies conducted for the primary purpose of facilitating information exchange across the public and private sectors are displayed in boxes in Figure 6-3. Other studies conducted for a different primary purpose, but which provided the secondary benefit of disseminating information, are displayed without boxes. This analysis show that the majority (14 studies) were primarily intended to provide information on life-cycle attributes.

Research, development, and demonstration. A secondary category of public policy orientation is RD&D (Figure 6-4). This category contains studies conducted as a research program to examine particular life-cycle attributes of the technology systems. The studies whose purpose was primarily RD&D are shown in boxes. Those where research function was secondary to the study's intent are

SETAC Press

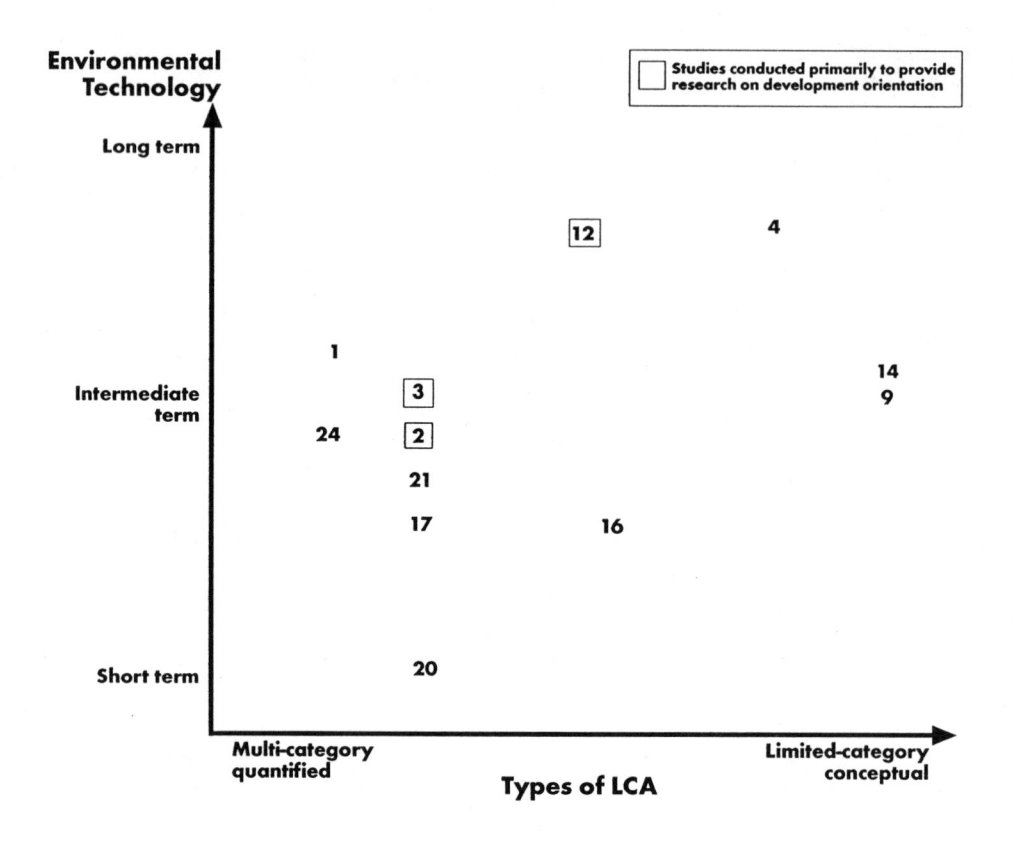

Figure 6-4   Research, development, and demonstration orientation

not enclosed. Only 3 of the 24 studies examined were deemed to serve as a tool for making decisions about RD&D funding. Two of these (numbers 2 and 3) represent recent Swedish studies and the third (number 12) is DOE's study of biomass-to-ethanol conversion. Nine additional studies were considered to serve a valuable contribution to the RD&D policy area as well.

Market stimulation. The third policy category is market simulation, referring to studies which served to promote a particular market (Figure 6-5). Usually, the markets involved some form of pollution reduction, control or prevention, recycling, or use of alternative energy sources. While the purpose of most private sector studies can be related to market incentive, it is apparent that approximately half of the government studies (11) also played an important role in guiding economic development of environmental technologies. This was true even though the stimulation of new markets was not considered the primary purpose of these studies.

Chapter 6: Environmental Technology

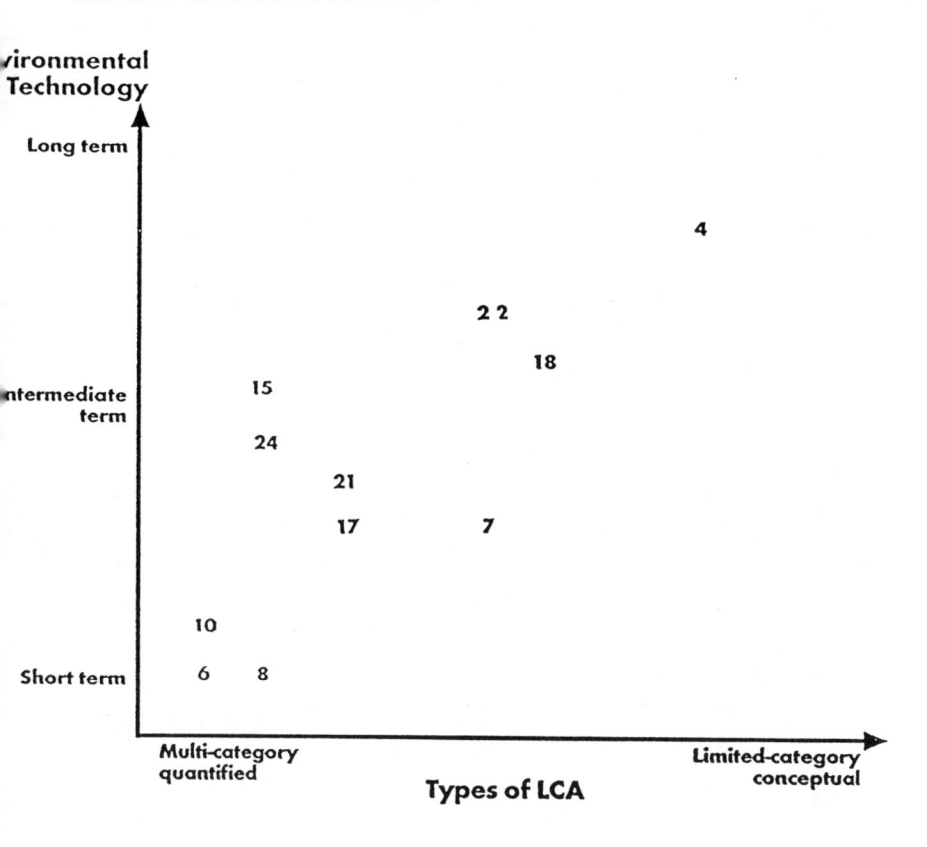

Figure 6-5 Market stimulation orientation

Regulatory. The fourth policy category identified in this analysis included studies (shown in boxes in Figure 6-6) that directly impacted regulatory policy. All 6 studies (4 Swedish, 1 French, 1 German) indicate the tendency of these governments to enact legislation pertaining to life-cycle attributes of products. In particular, the "extended producer responsibility" regulations of these countries provide powerful incentives for the application of LCA in both the public and private sector.

Other. The three additional areas of public policy orientation examined - fiscal policy, international commerce, and education and training - were largely devoid of LCA applications among the 24 studies examined. This may be due to the reliance on other management tools for these policy areas, as well as the uncertainty among policy-makers as to the benefits that LCA approaches can provide. While no studies were identified as having a primary purpose directed toward education and training, virtually all of the studies examined could be and perhaps have been applied toward this goal.

SETAC Press

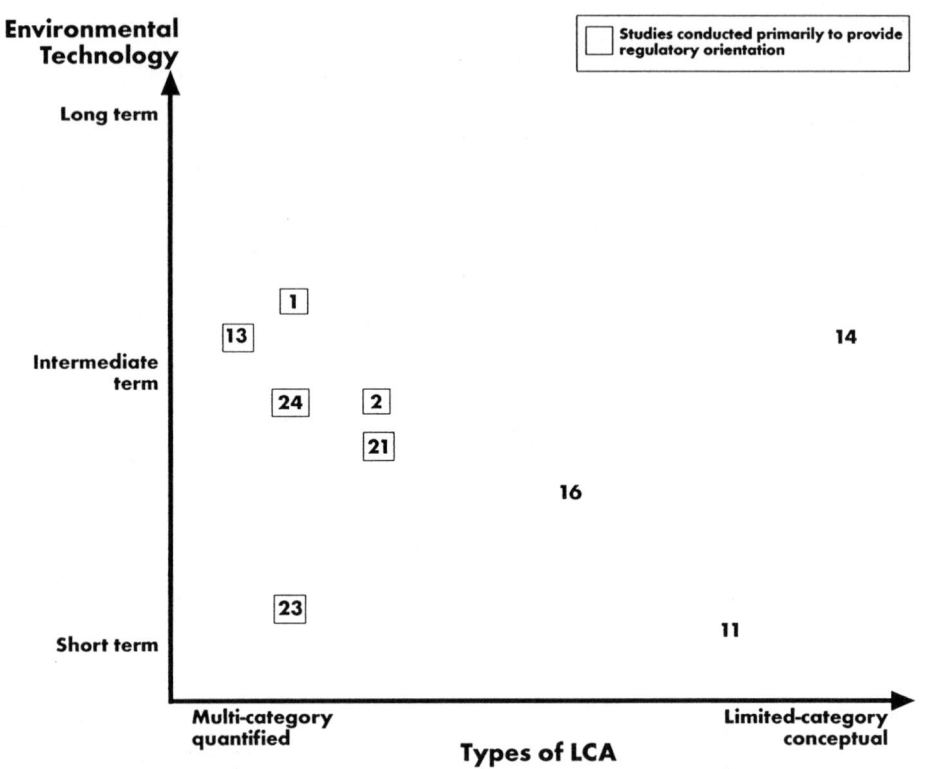

Figure 6-6 Regulatory orientation

6.4.5 Key Findings

The key findings from this analysis is that LCA studies to date have focused on 1) relatively short- to intermediate-term technological innovations and 2) relatively descriptive and quantitative approaches or formats. The need is clear. LCA can be expanded toward higher-level, longer-term technology innovations that reveal and even direct the development of new technology alternatives.

The second direction in which LCA can be expanded is toward applications involving more conceptual, more constitutive, broad-based planning. In fact, "LCA thinking," scoping, and holistic planning are essential to any movement toward higher level technological innovation, as the complexity and uncertainty involved in technology replacement virtually precludes a highly quantitative analysis.

> "Life-cycle analysis can help us understand the full cost, potential, and impact of new products and their associated technologies. As a systems approach, life-cycle analysis examines the entire set of environmental consequences of a product, including those that result from its manufacture, use, and disposal. Because the relationships among industrial processes are complex, life-cycle analysis requires sophisticated understanding of material flows, resource reuse, and product substitution. Shifting to an approach that considers all resources, products, and waste as an interdependent system will take time, but government can facilitate the shift by encouraging the transition to a systems approach."
>
> Technology for a Sustainable Future: A Framework for Action National Science and Technology Council. July 1994.
>
> The flow of materials and products through the world economy has a critical influence on both economic growth and the environment. These flows are determined in part by design decisions. Therefore, policy-makers should strive to make green product design an integral part of strategies to improve competitiveness and environmental quality....To move ahead, the environmental costs of production, consumption, and disposal should be accounted for at each stage of the product life cycle.

6.5 References

Cortese AD. 1992. Education for an environmentally sustainable future. *Environmental Science & Technology* 26(6):1108.

Executive Order 12873. October 20, 1993. Federal acquisition, recycling, and waste prevention.

[NSTC] U.S. National Science and Technology Council. Technology for a Sustainable Future, Office of Science and Technology Policy, Executive Office of the President, Washington, DC, 1994.

U.S. Congress. October 1992. Green products by design: choices for a cleaner environment. Washington DC: Office of Technology Assessment. OTA-E-541. p 86.

SETAC

A Professional Society for Environmental Scientists and Engineers and Related Disciplines Concerned with Environmental Quality

The Society of Environmental Toxicology and Chemistry (SETAC), with offices in North America and Europe, is a nonprofit, professional society that provides a forum for individuals and institutions engaged in the study of environmental problems, management and regulation of natural resources, education, research and development, and manufacturing and distribution.

Goals

- Promote research, education, and training in the environmental sciences
- Promote systematic application of all relevant scientific disciplines to the evaluation of chemical hazards
- Participate in scientific interpretation of issues concerned with hazard assessment and risk analysis
- Support development of ecologically acceptable practices and principles
- Provide a forum for communication among professionals in government, business, academia, and other segments of society involved in the use, protection, and management of our environment

Activities

- Annual meetings with study and workshop sessions, platform and poster papers, and achievement and merit awards
- Monthly scientific journal, *Environmental Toxicology and Chemistry*, SETAC newsletter, and special technical publications
- Funds for education and training through the SETAC Scholarship/Fellowship Program
- Chapter forums for the presentation of scientific data and for the interchange and study of information about local concerns
- Advice and counsel to technical and nontechnical persons through a number of standing and ad hoc committees

Membership

SETAC's growing membership includes more than 5,000 individuals from government, academia, business, and public-interest groups with technical backgrounds in chemistry, toxicology, biology, ecology, atmospheric sciences, health sciences, earth sciences, and engineering.

If you have training in these or related disciplines and are engaged in the study, use, or management of environmental resources, SETAC can fulfill your professional affiliation needs. Membership categories include Associate, Student, Senior Active, and Emeritus.

For more information, contact SETAC, 1010 North 12th Avenue, Pensacola, Florida, T 850 469 1500, F 850 469 9778, E setac@setac.org.

Other SETAC Life-Cycle Assessment Titles

A Conceptual Framework for Life-Cycle Impact Assessment, edited by Jim Fava, Frank Consoli, Richard Denison, Kenneth Dickson, Tim Mohin, Bruce Vigon

Guidelines for Life-Cycle Assessment: A "Code of Practice", edited by Frank Consoli, David Allen, Ian Boustead, James Fava, William Franklin, Allan Jensen, Nick de Oude, Rod Parrish, Rod Perriman, Dennis Postlethwaite, Beth Quay, Jacinthe Seguin, Bruce Vigon

Life-Cycle Assessment Data Quality: A Conceptual Framework, edited by Jim Fava, Allan Jensen, Lars Lindfors, Steven Pomper, Bea De Smet, John Warren, Bruce Vigon

A Technical Framework for Life-Cycle Assessment, edited by James A. Fava, Richard Denison, Bruce Jones, Mary Ann Curran, Bruce Vigon, Susan Selke, James Barnum